Welcoming
the Stranger

Welcoming the Stranger

*A Public Theology
of Worship and Evangelism*

Patrick R. Keifert

FORTRESS PRESS   MINNEAPOLIS

WELCOMING THE STRANGER
A Public Theology of Worship and Evangelism

All Scripture quotations, unless otherwise noted, are from the New Revised Standard Version of the Bible, copyright © 1989 by the Division of Christian Education of the National Council of Churches of Christ in the United States of America.

Cover design: Hilber Nelson

Library of Congress Cataloging-in-Publication Data

Keifert, Patrick R., 1950–
    Welcoming the stranger : a public theology of worship and
evangelism / Patrick R. Keifert.
        p.   cm.
    Includes bibliographical references.
    ISBN 0-8006-2492-0 (alk. paper)
    1. Public worship.   2. Evangelistic work.   I. Title.
BV15.K44   1992
264'.001—dc20   91-14231
                                                                                    CIP

The paper used in this publication meets the minimum requirements of American National Standard for Information Sciences—Permanence of Paper for Printed Library Materials, ANSI Z329.48-1984.   ∞™

Manufactured in the U.S.A.   AF 1-2492
96   95   94   93   92   1   2   3   4   5   6   7   8   9   10

In gratitude to

Ella F. (Rogers) Keifert
and
Erma F. (Larsen) Rogers

Contents

Preface

This book explores the public character of Christian thought and life in a culture of pluralism. It develops a public theology by coupling things that common sense generally separates: liturgical renewal and effective evangelism; evangelism and respect for cultural diversity; theory and practice. It unites them within the biblical metaphor of hospitality to the stranger, a theme that, either explicitly or implicitly, is present throughout.

I argue that if the church develops a public theology and practice within such a metaphor, it can harness the powerful resources of liturgical and evangelical renewal. Thus equipped, the church can meet the dual challenges in American culture of (1) the present spiritual awakening and (2) the moral demand to respect cultural and religious diversity. Working within the metaphor of hospitality to the stranger, Christians can respect the uniqueness of individuals and different cultures in America and can effectively proclaim the uniqueness of Christian faith and thought, especially the Christian liturgy and the apostolic commission to make disciples of all nations. Bringing such odd couples together requires more than the argument of this book; such synergy finally depends upon the Holy Spirit.

Providentially, the Spirit is working overtime in the 1990s, opening up more and more people to considering matters religious and theological. The Spirit is casting these people with their religious and theological questions into public space and causing the church, where it is still open to such conversation, to respond. One of the public spaces into which the Spirit is casting these seekers is public worship. While

I tend to think the church is often at its most inhospitable in public worship, the Spirit nevertheless draws them there. Those churches that respond with hospitality will enjoy growth at many levels, including numerical. Those who exclude these seekers and refuse to take up the challenge of public ministry among strangers will experience the opposite.

For the method and content for putting these topics together, I am deeply indebted to the work of two schools that supposedly do not go together—those at Chicago and at Yale. Personally, I am indebted to David Tracy and Paul Ricoeur, my dissertation advisers, and Langdon Gilkey and Martin E. Marty, all central figures in the Chicago School, and to Hans Frei and George Lindbeck, central figures of the Yale School.

As to the odd couple of theory and practice, this book is clearly practical in its purpose;[1] that is, it wishes to change directly the understanding and behavior of churches as they worship and evangelize. Its underlying concern is to educate Christian imagination and vision. To this end, it both draws from practical experience and situations and uses certain theories borrowed from theology, philosophy, sociology, psychology, and cultural anthropology.

Although my ends are practical, this book is not a how-to book; such a volume will follow. This book is an exercise in systematic theology, even as I focus on the church as my primary audience. I also hope to reach persons who are skeptical of Christian interest in both liturgical and evangelization renewal. Through the metaphor of hospitality to the stranger, I hope to show that these Christian interests are compatible with respect for religious and cultural diversity.

Along the way, I have received considerable and helpful criticism from a number of people. These include student assistants Carolyn McCrary Keller, Susan Leithe, Richard Swanson, Judith Stack, Michael Stade, Arlynne Turnquist, and Bryan Woken; and parish pastors and musicians Stephen Cornils, Gerald Hoffman, Steven McKinley, Merv Thompson, Richard Webb, and Donald Wisner. A number of colleagues have read and given suggestions: Carl Braaten, Gerhard Forde, Gracia Grindal, Richard Jensen, Donald Juel, Mary Knutsen, Martin E. Marty, Mark Oldenberg, Frank Senn, Mons Teig, and Paul Westemeyer. In addition to these colleagues, two others, Marie Failinger and Henry Horn, have offered vision, critique, and editorial suggestions far beyond my ability to thank them.

Many of the ideas forming this manuscript arose from the good advice given and experience gained from a number of congregations that have allowed me to serve them in some pastoral capacity. These include Mount Olive Lutheran, Minneapolis; Windsor Park Lutheran, Chicago; Pilgrim Evangelical Lutheran, Chicago; Trinity Lutheran, Cody, Wyoming; Hope Lutheran, Powell, Wyoming; Lord of Life, Renton, Washington; and, all in Minnesota, Galilee Lutheran, Roseville; Prince of Peace Lutheran, Burnsville; and Nativity Lutheran, St. Anthony.

The research that led to this manuscript was made possible by the generous sabbatical policy at Luther Northwestern Theological Seminary and the Franklin Clark Frye Post-Graduate Fellowship, sponsored by Aid Association for Lutherans. They made feasible a year of study and writing as a guest of the Institute for Ecumenical Research and the Protestant Faculty of the University of Tübingen. At the hands of the institute's director, Hans Küng, and the dean of the faculty at that time, Jürgen Moltmann, I enjoyed remarkable hospitality to the stranger. A special word of thanks for hospitality and support of this work, both during this study year and subsequently, goes to Michael Welker and his wife, Ulrika, then of the University of Tübingen, now of the University of Heidelberg.

Many thanks to my wife, Jeanette, and our daughters, Danielle, Johanna, and Sandra, especially Sandra, who has heard parts of this manuscript many, many times. Finally, I dedicate this book to my mother, Ella F. Rogers Keifert, and my grandmother, Erma F. Larsen Rogers, who evangelized me primarily through their faithful attending of worship and explaining its truth, meaning, and meaningfulness for them and for me.

Introduction:
Public Worship
and the Stranger

When I was serving my pastoral internship, I visited many people who lived within our parish area but who were not members of any congregation. Barbara Whiterabbit (not her real name) was one of these persons. Her name and address were given to me by a school social worker who was concerned that Barbara, a single parent, might be abusing her children.

On my first visit to Barbara's home, I was afraid of what might happen. I hesitated at the bottom of the long staircase that led to her second-floor flat. Several steps were broken through, so I had to step carefully over them. I wondered anxiously how Barbara would receive me. Would I only make things worse for her and her children? Would my presence as a clergyman only intensify the blame-guilt cycle that led to child abuse in this home? I was so unsure of myself that if she had slammed the door in my face, I would have been relieved. But she let me in.

I explained that I was the student pastor from a local church and that I was trying to get to know the people of the neighborhood. Much to my surprise, she was willing to talk and invited me to sit down at her kitchen table. We chatted for quite a while, mostly about her struggle to make ends meet and her hopes to qualify for some aid so she could become a licensed practical nurse. I promised to look into some possible sources for financial help, which I eventually found for her.

That first conversation led to many others, always at her home. After several weeks, I asked if she wanted her children to come to weekday church school—among other things, they would get a free hot meal, and she would have some free time in the evening. She agreed. Later, Barbara's children joined the congregation's Sunday school.

Then one day, on her own initiative, Barbara asked if we could meet at my office the next time. "Sure," I responded eagerly. When the day came, she arrived right on time. I suspect that she took an early bus so she would be prompt and then shyly waited outside somewhere. Although she did not attend church, she wore her best "Sunday" dress clothes.

After a short conversation about the building and my room, she blurted out, "I think I would like to go to church here some Sunday."

"Well," said I, surprised and somewhat proud, "of course! What we do on Sunday is open to the public."

"Could we go into the place where you have your service?" she asked tentatively. "I kind of want to get used to things before I come for the real thing."

"A good idea," I responded. She obviously had been thinking ahead.

We went into the space for worship. It was dark, mysterious (even to me), and awe inspiring. We sat down about halfway up. Thinking it might help to go through the service with her, I took out the hymnal and opened to the service of Holy Communion. As I began to talk about the service and what would happen on Sunday morning, I knew I was in trouble. She tightened in fear; her spirit became angry. Her face told me that she felt like a complete foreigner in this place. She asked, "Will I have to do all of this Sunday morning?"

Our conversations had always been in the places where she lived her life, with me always struggling to be at home in that space. Now, in a few minutes' time, she had moved from that safe space to my office, and then to this dark, mysterious place that was mine. And I, whom she had trusted, was whispering strange, threatening, and—to her—nonsensical words and was miming the actions that are intended to be liturgy, the work of the people.

I cared about Barbara and wanted to share with her this marvelous world of mine. But what was for me sheer delight, the receiving of the gifts of God and my response of praise and thanksgiving, was for her the tradition of an ethnic ghetto. The liturgy within which my grandmother and mother had nurtured me from infancy was foreign for Barbara, the "tradition of men." The tears stung in my eyes.

The term "tradition of men" came to mind because earlier that day, as I was preparing a class on Mark's Gospel, I read Jesus' blistering response to the Pharisees.

The Pharisees and the scribes asked him, "Why do your disciples not live according to the tradition of the elders, but eat with defiled hands?" He said to them, "Isaiah prophesied rightly about you hypocrites, as it is written,

> 'This people honors me with their lips,
>   but their hearts are far from me;
> in vain do they worship me,
>   teaching human precepts as doctrines.'

You abandon the commandment of God and hold to human tradition [KJV: the tradition of men]." (Mark 7:5-8)

My meetings with Barbara came as an unexpected gift, an opportunity to respond to her fundamental human needs and to share the gospel, one to another. Fortunately, these opportunities are common; unfortunately, so are the tensions such as those that arose in the encounter between Barbara Whiterabbit and me in the worship space.

What is uncommon about our encounter, as recent studies have shown, is that Barbara Whiterabbit deliberately sought me out and wanted to learn about our worship practices before she attended worship. Unlike the pattern in the three decades after World War II, when people typically sought out pastors or congregational members before they came to church, most unchurched visitors in the 1980s made their first formal contacts with the institutional church as unannounced visitors to "check out" Sunday morning worship services.[1]

As a result, Sunday morning worship has become a moment of evangelism whether Christians like it or not—indeed, whether they are prepared or not. The critical question is thus not whether we will choose to do evangelism but whether the challenge of evangelism that is thrust upon us is being effectively met.

In my observation of a wide variety of congregations, the evangelistic responses to this challenge of the uninvited visitor are startlingly diverse. Some congregations simply choose to ignore the new challenge, believing that the tactics of the sixties and seventies are sufficient to respond to those who come as strangers in the 1990s.

Other pastors and parishioners believe that worship and evangelism do not belong together. For these congregational members worship is primarily the care and nurture of the congregational family, a time for bonding and communication, much like time around a family dinner table. Evangelism, by contrast, is a form of private salesmanship for the worship "product," an activity that is important but is best carried on through one-on-one contacts outside the worship hour. For those who wish to separate the two, the evangelist's task is finished once he or she gets a skeptic to "buy," that is, to pass through the church portals a few times. To speak of blending worship and evangelism simply confuses matters for them; it blurs the lines between the public, out-in-the-world solicitation of evangelism and the private, in-here-with-the-family nurturing of worship, and thus it lessens the effectiveness of both activities.

Still other Christians firmly hold that evangelism and worship do not mix because worship, the liturgy, is a fragile heritage that successful evangelism may threaten. As a tradition, the liturgy must be handed down intact and with great care, so as not to lose the strength and truth of the gospel preserved in the liturgy. These liturgical traditionalists are by no means naive; in fact, they often have a keen sense of the contemporary malaise in American culture. Responding to the threats from without, they seek to provide a secure place for Christians against the danger this malaise poses to much that they hold to be good, beautiful, and true.

Finally, still other congregations, or sometimes just a few of their members, perceive the challenge of the unannounced visitor as an opportunity. They believe good worship is itself effective evangelism. These congregations seek to design Sunday morning liturgies that can connect the churched and the unchurched, that can evangelize members and visitors alike. These evangelists are pragmatic when it comes to worship and have little time for what they perceive to be elitist liturgical agendas.

While those who respond to the challenge of worship and evangelism might disagree on how to respond, they would all essentially agree on how one should interpret the encounter Barbara Whiterabbit and I had in the space for worship. Each of these groups would say that our encounter only demonstrates the common wisdom that liturgical worship and effective evangelism do not work well together in a pluralistic culture.

Those who agree with this view see the congregation's choice as either-or. They hold that a congregation must choose between faithful liturgical worship or effective evangelism, that if a congregation wants to evangelize, either it must radically change the liturgy to make evangelism successful, or it must leave evangelism to other times and places, or even to other congregations.

But is the common wisdom correct? Before any congregation either discards its liturgy or gives up on evangelism, it should examine this received wisdom about worship and evangelism more carefully.

In this book I show, contrary to common wisdom, that liturgical
worship and effective evangelism can complement and enhance one
another. By "liturgical worship," I mean worship consistent with the
historic public liturgy of the Christian church whereby "the full, conscious, and active participation" of the people takes place.[2] This definition of liturgical worship is in explicit contrast to worship understood
as "presentation evangelism," which leaves people passive observers of
a few who seek to evangelize them.[3]

I understand effective evangelism as proclaiming the good news and
leading people to a public identity in Christ. It is a direct address that
makes present in the life of the addressee the liberating presence of the
triune God and leads them to a public identification with that God
through Christ. It is "not the same as inviting people to unite with a
specific congregation and welcoming them into the nurturing fellowship
of that worshiping congregation,"[4] even though the process of welcoming and receiving new members needs to be coordinated with effective
evangelism.

Many congregations are quite adept at proclaiming the gospel but
very inept at welcoming and assimilating people. Others may be very
successful at welcoming and receiving new members but seldom proclaim the gospel. Neither are aptly organized to lead people to a public
identification with the triune God since both focus on making members,
not Christians or disciples. Effective evangelism does both.

Effective evangelism and liturgical worship belong together in a mutual apostolic mission. As stated before, this belief is in sharp contrast
to the common wisdom that sees liturgical and evangelical renewal as
incompatible. This belief is justified, however, once we understand two
sets of assumptions that underlie the contemporary wisdom and contrast
these assumptions with the biblical tradition of worship and evangelism.

The first chapters uncover the assumptions behind the common wisdom and reflect on how these assumptions distort the way we experience,
and reflect on, Christian public worship and evangelism. In the second
half of the volume, I propose that congregations discard their either-
or way of thinking about worship and evangelism and instead adopt a
"both-and" approach to integrating liturgical worship and effective evangelism.

More precisely, my proposal involves a pastoral-theological strategy
for integrating the two. By the term "pastoral," I do not mean "for
clergy only"; rather, it is for all persons who are publicly responsible
for the care and nurture of the church's life, especially worship and

evangelism. Thus, I invite members of worship committees, liturgists, church musicians, evangelists, those preparing for these offices, as well as clergy to reflect with me.

The proposal is also theological. It holds that the logic of worship is grounded neither in tradition nor in practical novelty but rather in God and the presence and actions of God in worship; it is a theologic.[5] This makes the argument I set forth somewhat unusual, since discussions between "liturgical traditionalists" and "practical evangelists" seldom develop around a theological center. Too often in such dialogue, significant theological questions are ignored in favor of intense arguments over questions of historicity and favorable marketing strategies. These discussions, which can be heated, often neglect important questions such as how God is present and active in public life generally, and in Christian public worship specifically.

Third, this is a strategic proposal. Its determined focus is on the long-term aims of pastoral ministry rather than on quick-fix tactics for gaining large numbers of new members. Its aim, nonetheless, is decidedly practical, in the sense that it hopes to change the behavior and effectiveness of church leaders and congregations. It hopes, however, to do this by addressing their imaginations and practical reasoning skills, by providing a diagnosis of their present situation, rather than providing a list of surefire recipes for growth. It shares Lyle E. Schaller's conviction that "most people have a greater capability to overcome obstacles, to solve problems, and to change the conditions they are confronted with than they give themselves credit for possessing. Frequently, however, people need help in diagnosing problems and in distinguishing between symptoms and problems."[6]

This proposal is directed at those who are interested in and committed to congregational growth in mission. To some extent, it sees the church-growth movement as an ally in this strategic proposal. Thus, the proposal encourages congregations to strive toward effective worship and evangelism ministry that positions them for growth. It believes that unless congregations plan to grow, they probably will not grow.

In terms of theories of church growth, I share with Carl George, the director of the Fuller Institute for Church Growth, the conviction that liturgical worship deployed within a mission-oriented strategy can be an aid to growth in mission.[7] Along with George, this book rejects the temptation to reduce all worship to "entertainment evangelism," without rejecting the place of presentation evangelism within worship settings. It also challenges those congregations who wish to retain their liturgical heritage to wake up from their present lethargy toward their apostolic commission to share the gospel with all peoples. Whatever else it means to be apostolic, it surely means to be sent as evangelical witnesses to the fate and ministry of Jesus Christ and to carry out the plan of God among the nations.[8]

In support of planning for growth in mission, this pastoral-theological strategy proposes tactics not just for creating but also for effectively serving large numbers of people, placing such tactics within a broad, long-term pastoral-theological strategy. These tactics for this theological strategy can be planned by congregations large and small, rural, urban, and suburban.[9] Although much of the historical work cited in this text is drawn from urban studies, recent rural sociology indicates that the relevant social and psychological patterns of city life are also present in country congregations and parishioners. Some of my suggestions may work better in a large urban or town-and-country parishes, others in small rural or suburban parishes. Yet, the examples in the book come from a wide variety of congregations, and though not all suggestions and examples will apply to each congregation, the underlying principles surely do.[10]

The sources used to develop the pastoral-theological strategy of this book include (1) Christian tradition, particularly the biblical tradition of public worship and hospitality to the stranger; (2) studies of modern culture—specifically, analyses of modern American public life and the role of ritual in contemporary cultures of pluralism; and (3) the Christian faith experience (both personal and communal), especially the attempts of contemporary Christians to keep faith with their heritage of public worship within pluralistic cultures.

As abstract as these sources might initially appear, the entire strategy of this book actually grows out of the day-to-day ministry experience of many pastors and church workers like myself. Indeed, personal experiences, such as mine with Barbara, serve as more than anecdotes in this strategy attempting to integrate liturgical worship and effective evangelism. These narratives set the context for research of Scripture, tradition, and culture. Out of such personal experiences and my own reading of the Scriptures, I draw the primary metaphor that links liturgical worship and effective evangelism in this text: *hospitality to the stranger.*

This metaphor is woven throughout Barbara's encounter with me, and mine with her. My initial fear about visiting Barbara, a stranger to me, is resolved by her hospitality. Barbara first hosts me, and then I host her. The re-creation of the roles of host and guest, and the constant reversal of such roles, characterizes not just our own narrative but also most evangelical encounters.

When we moderns talk of showing hospitality to the stranger, however, we usually mean that we strive to allow the stranger into our private worlds for the moment, to make the stranger feel at home. In this popular understanding of hospitality, if the stranger does not become a friend, we have not been successful in our hospitality.

The cozy images of friendship at the hearth or the family table, however, do not do justice to our real experiences of attempting to show hospitality to strangers, particularly in public settings. In our own lives, whether we are considering picking up a hitchhiker or inviting prospective in-laws to dinner, we soon discover that we are endangered. Not all strangers are safe. Perhaps even more important for this discussion, strangers more often than not remain strangers, even when we are good hosts.

When we speak of public worship, however, we should not conclude that our hospitality has failed simply because we have failed to make these strangers our friends or to make a safe place for both us and them. Rather, we have failed only in creating certain sentimentalized relationships that are often characterized as hospitality in the contemporary Western world. In the church, showing hospitality to a stranger is less a matter of making the stranger feel at home and more a matter of opening one's private world to the stranger. In fact, it is a matter of opening one's private world to a public one, of gaining the competence to participate in the customs of public life, of learning to enjoy life among strangers.

Indeed, the response of hospitality to the stranger can by no means be limited to the specific one-on-one friendly encounters we usually imagine by this metaphor. Hospitality to the stranger is critical to public life by definition, because it is precisely the interaction of strangers through a common set of actions that constitutes a public.[11] Where there is no space for strangers, there can be no public.

In discussing a strategy of hospitality in the church that can constitute a public, I use the term "stranger" in three senses. One group of strangers to the church, those who are like Barbara, are clearly outsiders.[12] Often, they may dress and speak differently from congregational members; they may well be of a different class, race, age, or life situation than the so-called insiders. In fact, the very fact that they have entered church for the first time may mark them obviously as different.

Most people gathered for public worship in the church, however, are not such obvious outside strangers. Yet they remain outside the intimate group that usually makes up most of the leadership in a congregation. This second group of strangers—the "inside" strangers—fits somewhere between the intimate group, or family leaders of the congregation, and the outsiders. If they desire to participate meaningfully in public worship, they face many, though not all, of the obstacles that Barbara faces. And the same social and psychological elements that shamed Barbara away from worship will cause them to be members of a passive audience, rather than active participants, on Sunday morning.

I will also use the term "stranger" in the sense of the irreducible difference between two persons that exists in any encounter. This irreducible difference is most obvious with outside strangers, less obvious with inside strangers, and even less noticeable with those with whom we have regular contact. Nonetheless, even with our closest friends and family members, there remains an irreducible difference. They remain in significant ways strangers. This irreducible difference also exists in our ability to know ourselves. In this third sense, we remain, even to ourselves, strangers.

In terms of congregational analysis, these inside strangers as well as outsiders like Barbara will remain outside as long as we continue to relate the public and private spheres of our lives in accordance with two modern assumptions, what I will call undercurrents in contemporary life. They are truly undercurrents because they seldom rise explicitly to the surface of our discussions of liturgy and evangelism, but they profoundly affect how we understand and experience both.

In the first chapter, I analyze the first of these undercurrents: the ideology of intimacy. I begin by describing the social and psychological dynamics of public life and how they characterize our public worship. Once these dynamics are exposed, it will be clear how the ideology of intimacy causes us to exclude others, even when we are sure that we are including them.

In the second chapter, I move to the second and more profound of these modern undercurrents: the ideology of individualism and the separation of the public and the private. As I will develop in more detail, the contemporary separation of our public and private worlds depends on our eagerness to segregate facts from values: to believe that reality is split between the small number of objectively provable facts that govern how we live our public lives, and a massive number of subjective (indeed, relative) values, which should be kept within our private lives.

Religion, whose truth claims can only with difficulty be objectively proved as "facts," is thus relegated to private life. With other significant human values and experiences, it is thus walled out of public life and trivialized as a matter of taste.[13]

The undercurrents of individualism and the separation of the public and the private flow together to create an eddy of pastoral-theological strategies that focus on the private sphere. After all, reasons the modern person, if religion properly belongs to the private sphere, then our pastoral-theological strategies should mimic the tactics that have worked successfully in other private-sphere matters, such as the constitution of the family. Thus, it is tempting to idealize intimate contact and intense, long-term relationships as the models for effective ministry. Public ministry—ministry among and for strangers—is at best demoted and at worst set aside.

Most of our congregations, because they limit their ministry to these private pastoral-theological strategies, function as "single-cell churches."[14] They imagine themselves as one extended family and limit both the number and variety of people they can care for and involve in their congregational life by so imagining themselves.[15]

Single-cell churches rarely have more than 200 or 250 people in attendance on a given Sunday morning, regardless of their membership list.[16] They tend to devalue the public nature of the liturgy and turn it into the worship of their extended family. Both liturgy as public worship and evangelism as public witness to the gospel suffer in private pastoral-theological strategies. Thus, proponents both of faithful liturgy and of eager evangelism have something to gain by recognizing the effect of these undercurrents on contemporary pastoral-theological strategy.

Although the church is profoundly affected by these two undercurrents, a church that can resist their force by trusting God's promise in the gospel can bridge rather than separate the public and private spheres. In fact, sociologists like Parker Palmer have persuasively argued that the church can itself help to create and enliven public life. As a "school of the spirit" in which people mature as active members of the public, the church can be a very important bridge between the private and the public in contemporary life.[17]

I share Palmer's optimism that we can reconstruct the relationship of the public and the private in our society, and that public worship, though only one of the many bridges between public and private, is for Christians the ideal bridge. Public worship, where the gospel is proclaimed and embodied, both shapes and models how the Christian relates all aspects of public and private life.

Yet those, like Palmer, who have envisioned an important new role for the church in community life have not adequately reflected on or articulated a theory of Christian public worship that can sustain this role.[18] Not only a theory of public worship that focuses on theology but also some exploration of the practice and planning of public worship based on that theory need articulation.

A first step in understanding and relating the theory and practice of worship and evangelism in contemporary culture is to focus on the importance of ritual in enlivening public life. Ritual's importance has been sensed, in the modern period, by one group of Christians more than others: the liturgical renewers. The third chapter reviews the liturgical renewal movements of this century, showing how they tried to respond to the rejection of ritual and how their considerable success in restoring ritual to its essential role in public worship was marred when they succumbed to the modern undercurrents they so sought to counteract. As a result, much of liturgical renewal remained mired in the bog of personal taste, of relativistic private views. Rather than opening Christian worship to the stranger, the rites of the liturgical renewal primarily confused and excluded the stranger, a most unfortunate but not inevitable result.

As I argue in the rest of the book, reconstruction of the relationship between the public and private dimensions of our lives begins when we reconstruct our public worship. Reconstruction does not mean that we should either repristinate past visions or ignore them. Rather, it means that we must attend to the realities of religious freedom, pluralism, and the potential conflict and oppressive behavior among strangers in contemporary culture while we trust the essential wisdom of the biblical tradition.

In the fourth chapter I trace this biblical tradition, describing how both ancient Israel and the early church framed public worship using the metaphor of hospitality to the stranger. The understanding that this metaphor captures grew from their belief that God was the ultimate Host of public worship and that all worshipers were dependent upon God's hospitality. For the early church, as for us, it is from God's hospitality that our calling to be hospitable grows; we are thereby impelled to emphasize specially the public dimension of worship. In the early church this public emphasis led to a twofold pastoral-theological strategy for worship and evangelism—residential worship and itinerant preaching services—a strategy adaptable even for today.

In chapter 5, on the basis of the biblical vision, I propose the first part of a pastoral-theological strategy for public worship in a culture of pluralism. I begin by rebutting the ideology of intimacy and imagining the church, following Parker Palmer's image, as a company of strangers.

In the sixth chapter, I follow the evangelical and Episcopal theologian Robert Webber in calling for a "liturgical evangelism" as the second part of this strategy. Such evangelism "calls a person into Christ and the church through a conversion regulated and ordered by worship. These conversion-directed services order the inner experience of repentance from sin, faith in Christ, transformation of one's life, and entrance into the Christian community."[19]

In accordance with the Scriptures, liturgical evangelism holds that hospitality to strangers is not a peripheral matter in Christian public worship but in fact is central. Through such liturgical evangelism, conversion grows beyond a private experience to a public event by which individuals gain a public Christian identity. Liturgical evangelism bridges the private and public dimensions and enhances both.

Following the biblical tradition of hospitality, the pastoral-theological strategy outlined in this book thus calls for two relatively different orders of Christian public worship, much like early Christians distinguished between house worship and itinerant preaching. Just as a sports team plays differently on its home field than it does when it is traveling, I will suggest that we develop both "at home" and "away" public worship tactics. Such a strategy takes seriously the idea that public worship is evangelical outreach and that contemporary persons need a public ritual they can understand and join. It also takes seriously the place of public worship as the nurturing of the faithful, old and new, for service and witness in the world.

It is not enough to know that ritual contributes to effective evangelism and public life. The importance of ritual to effective evangelism requires some sense of how ritual affects our interaction with each other. In chapter 7 I describe why ritual hospitality is an essential part of our pastoral-theological strategy.

In chapter 8 I develop this concept of ritual as hospitality through various ritual strategies for public worship and explore the need for Christians to develop both ritual competence and ritual resourcefulness. Ritual competence is a person's ability to participate meaningfully, in a manner appropriate to his or her age and social status, in the traditional public ritual of the culture. Ritual resourcefulness is that person's ability to develop essential ritual competencies in a number of new and varied settings.

Even in a culture of pluralism, argues Roland Delattre, a professor of American studies, ritual competence remains an essential ingredient in making public life possible.[20] Both ritual competence and resourcefulness are necessary if we are to sustain public interaction that does not succumb to the modern undercurrents.

Christian worshipers can become ritually competent and resourceful only if worship leaders are attentive to these realities during the process of planning worship. The final two chapters propose a worship-planning process that recognizes, but is not ruled by, the modern undercurrents. Chapter 9 describes the public imagination that needs to pervade the process of planning worship. This public imagination begins with the acknowledgment of God's self-giving, self-sacrificing, liberating presence on behalf of and through the stranger.

Chapter 10 redescribes, in the setting of worship planning, the three basic sources for creating truly public worship. They are the same sources drawn upon in this book to describe the current situation and the church's response to it: tradition, culture, and faith experience. In this chapter I propose a process for worship planning that is infused with theological insights provided by the metaphor of hospitality. It integrates the planning of public worship with theological insights governed by hospitality to the stranger.

The pastoral-theological strategy for worship and evangelism outlined here sees these opportunities as complementary, not competitive. Liturgical renewal, characterized by hospitality to the stranger and ritual resourcefulness, creates a bridge between the public and the private over which the gospel can have free course. By means of this bridge, the church as a "school of the Spirit" matures in its ability to enliven the public life. Through those called into Christ through liturgical evangelism, it welcomes the stranger—who is, after all, each of us.

1

Public Worship in an Intimate Society

The encounter between Barbara Whiterabbit and me concerning the book of worship and the worship space appears to confirm the common wisdom that liturgical worship and effective evangelism do not go together well. The problem, according to this common wisdom, is with the worship liturgy. If we did away with the liturgy in favor of more intimate worship, Barbara and I would not have been shamed. If our worship were more spontaneous, it would give persons a chance to express their true feelings. If it were more relaxed and unplanned, then worship would be warmer and more open, a place where even outsiders would feel safe. In essence, this commonsense wisdom holds that each congregation needs to be an extended family, with worship that is family worship—intimate and loving rather than cold and impersonal.

If, according to this common wisdom, a congregation is not warm and intimate, it cannot be meaningful or real. And the church has an obligation, this wisdom holds, to create *real* communities in a world filled with pseudocommunities and harsh, empty public spaces—to create families and friends in a friendless void.

This common wisdom, however, makes for neither good worship nor effective evangelism. When we plan, practice, and evaluate public worship according to these intimate criteria, we in fact *reduce* the important and the real to only the private dimensions of our lives. We thereby accept what Parker Palmer calls the ideology of intimacy and actually contribute to the fall of public worship.[1] For the reality is that Barbara will not feel more welcome, should we turn Sunday morning into family worship. She does not need to become one of the family

15

in order to participate in worship. Nor should we allow the church to become one big happy family, if our worship is to be truly public.

This chapter asks, What are the dynamics of how public worship is experienced in contemporary society? It seeks answers in social and psychological studies, relying heavily on Richard Sennett's analysis of contemporary society, which he characterizes as "the intimate society."[2] The chapter suggests that in this society, the desire to make intimate what is primally public infects even the experience of worshipers in modern life.

The Intimate Society

The intimate society, according to Sennett, has developed over the last two hundred years, after the demise of the feudal system and the rise of the middle class. In an extensive description that goes beyond the scope of our task, Sennett shows how the broad forces of capitalism and secularism brought about the psychological dynamics characteristic of the intimate society. He isolates four social and psychological factors that clarify the reasons we tend to evaluate public worship in private, intimate terms.

In the intimate society, Sennett identifies (1) concern about the involuntary disclosure of character, (2) defense against such disclosure through withdrawal, (3) silence, and (4) the superimposition of private imagery upon the public. I add a fifth dynamic—fear of being shamed. A description of these five dynamics of the intimate society illustrates not only why we feel the way we do in worship but also how the forces of such a society tear apart and deform Christian worship and plague our attempts to restore its public dimension.

Involuntary Disclosure of Character

In many ways, the intimate society was the necessary adjustment of young people moving from rural settings to make their fortunes in the capitals of Europe, such as Paris and London. Sennett considers young rural folk encountering the multitudes in Paris or London in the first third of the nineteenth century. They are surrounded by people just like themselves, newcomers to the city; many are single or have young families; most are earning money for the first time in their lives. They are part of a great, unknown, ill-defined company of strangers.

Such young people would enter the city with few public signs of social position, but this would have been a fairly recent phenomenon. Shortly before this time, various styles of dress distinguished the various social classes in the city, which made social interaction possible without being forced into extensive personal disclosure. As this period in Sennett's story begins, however, the newcomers are left to their own devices because these signs of earlier periods were no longer meaningful or were signs of privilege and injustice. The question for them became how they could understand who they were and who all of the other strangers were.

All they could do was wait for the inevitable, fateful moment when another person's true character would be revealed by some slip of the tongue or some unintended clue from his or her manner of dress. The assumption is that an individual's genuine self will be involuntarily revealed, that one's real character is just waiting to overcome one's own efforts to keep it hidden. While he or she lies concealed, waiting for that moment, the watcher withdraws to a safe distance, covering himself or herself until others reveal their true character.

Defense through Withdrawal

If I imagine, for a moment, that I am a young person during this time and place myself into the position of the watcher, I can readily see the need for distance. If the stranger's character will be involuntarily revealed, then so will mine. If I locate myself among strangers, I need a safe place from which I can watch and wait. I also need to develop a style of speech and dress that hides from any unknowns who I am.

Out of this new urban situation emerged the Victorian manner of dress and speech, designed to suppress one's individuality. One dressed like everyone else, precisely to avoid exposing one's self, especially one's sexual desires and interests.

The search to uncover another's identity in the public place, however, did not end after everyone began to dress identically. Quite to the contrary, the careful observation of others only intensified. Now others sought and found differences not in obvious manners of dress but in minute details.

The dress of a gentleman of considerable means might not, upon first examination, look much different from that of the retail salesman who worked for him. To the discerning eye, however, minute details in stitching, tailoring, and type of cloth would reveal the true gentleman.

Naturally, the true gentleman would never point out these details, but he could readily tell which of his colleagues were of his class and which were not.

Women's dress was more circumscribed than men's. As time passed and this Victorian fear of the involuntary disclosure of character grew, so did the use of dress to repress sexuality and the attention to even more minute indications of personal character. While the fear of sexual desires was not uniquely Victorian, the unquestioned belief that one's sexuality could be disclosed through dress made this fear an obsession.

Though contemporary society has rejected the Victorian repression of sexuality, we have not similarly altered the assumptions that made it so powerful. For all our rebellion, we have not freed ourselves from focus upon individual personality in the public domain. Instead, we assume that our personal character will be involuntarily revealed through some Freudian slip. Indeed, we have simply turned the tables by assuming that we can control the expression of self by flaunting our sexuality and choosing an "image" through our dress.

We spend as much time "psyching out" others as the Victorians did looking for the tiny indications in dress that would reveal a person's true character. We understand clothes to be a sure sign of character and spend much of our time reading the personality of strangers from their clothes.[3]

Barbara's decision to wear Sunday-go-to-meeting clothes when she came to church may have indicated her desire to hide her individual character. Just so had my mother and grandmother invariably worn their cloth coats to church, especially on communion Sunday. The profound sense that at all costs they must cover themselves in this public place had little to do with their fear that God might see something, but rather with the concern that their neighbor might. Barbara and my mother and grandmother feared the painful exposure of the self to shame.

Fear of Being Shamed

Before considering the last two of Sennett's four dynamics, we discuss the sociopsychological dynamic of shame, the importance of which in the intimate society is only beginning to be understood.[4] Shame is as central to human experience as anxiety or suffering, developing strongest in the context of significant others, but also among strangers. It has not generally been the subject, however, of as much research or public conversation. One might even say that we have been ashamed of shame. Some scholars in the field of psychology have suggested that we live in a culture of shame.

Shame develops in the context of interpersonal relationships, most strongly in those with significant others, but also among strangers. In fact, the obsession with the self, which is characteristic of the psychology of the intimate society, can be understood as a part of the dynamic of shame in relationship to the fear of strangers.

Assuming that shame is a normal part of human experience, its place in the early stages of the intimate society can be assumed. It could explain the initial belief in the involuntary revelation of the self. Once this shaming affect placed the self in the center of consciousness, without accepted social barriers for the self to hide behind, the obsession of self-consciousness could easily follow. The dynamics of the shaming affect require more clarification, since they are an important ingredient in understanding the dynamics inhibiting the public character of Christian public worship.

When people feel ashamed, they feel as if they are being seen in a very diminished sense. They feel exposed to anyone who wants to look, to anyone who is present. They even feel as if they are small to themselves and are divided against themselves. Part of the person is looking down on himself or herself. This unexpected feeling of exposure and self-consciousness characterizes the experience of shame.

The person experiencing shame feels as if his or her whole self is being exposed to the all-knowing observation of others—and there is nothing one can do about it. Shame freezes one's ability to react. One feels naked and unable to find anything with which to cover oneself.

One is ashamed when no particular act but rather everything about one's self is seen as wrong. In the experience of shame, the whole person comes under the vision of an all-seeing eye. Sustained eye contact with others is extremely painful. One hangs one's head and is silenced. Not even the shame can be communicated. The person experiencing shame is then paralyzed.

Ashamed, the person becomes bound by self-consciousness. This dynamic of the self watching the self and looking down on the self binds the self. We find ourselves observing ourselves, almost glaring into our souls, and we find ourselves lacking, insufficient. We are naked before an awful judge, and that judge is ourselves. It is not so much that others are watching us, though indeed they may be, but that we are watching ourselves. We feel as if others are doing so and feel as if we are painfully exposed to others.

As I began to describe the worship service on Sunday morning, Barbara's body language revealed that she was ashamed. She withdrew into herself; the muscles around her lips became tight with strain; her eyes and head dropped. Once some time had passed, she reacted in a way that is common for those ashamed: she became angry. Her anger made it possible for her to break out of the shame that otherwise might have kept her self-bound. She felt that I had betrayed her. I seemed to have ignored the intimacy of our relationship, the mutual trust and security. Instead of protecting her, I was exposing her.

In turn, I felt exposed. I recognized that something was seriously wrong, that we were estranged. Although at the time I did not recognize her body language as expressing shame, I knew instinctively that the results of that shame—withdrawal, silence, and finally anger—were related to my breaking of the interpersonal bridge between us. Likewise, her reaction to the liturgy was a shaming experience for me. I felt immobilized by the feeling that I was being judged by her and even by myself. What was for me this intimate heritage from my mother and grandmother was for her the "tradition of men." Jesus' words regarding those who would put such a tradition before the commandments of God came back as a part of my reaction of shame.

Even if we had not been ashamed, we were both assuming that we might involuntarily disclose our character. The power of shame may exist in any culture and time, but it has a particular power in an intimate society obsessed either with controlling disclosure of character or with flaunting it.

Shame is an unavoidable human affect but becomes an obsession in a culture where public life is understood as the revelation or expression of self. Where individuals are not encouraged to use the vehicles of ritual and other conventions in the public place as instruments through which they might enjoy social interaction with strangers, shame and the fear of being shamed are likely to be prominent parts of public interaction.

Silence and the Audience

The power of shame in an intimate society is also evident in the next psychological dynamic characteristic of the intimate society: silence. Once again, imagine young persons arriving in the capital city to seek their fortune surrounded by others like themselves, unknowns without any shared public masks or rituals within which to function. Convinced that one's self and that of strangers will expose itself involuntarily, they withdraw into defensive silence. The defense of silence, which may either precede or accompany an affect of shame, would seem the most logical choice for someone denied the resources of social instruments and rituals.

Since one was acutely sensitive to intimate matters of selfhood and personality in the public space, one withdrew to work on one's own identity in protective, silent privacy. One became a spectator, an isolated figure, even in public. In silence, watching public life go by, a man (the respectable woman did not belong in the public place) was at last free.

But free for what? Free to pursue personal identity but not social interchange or mutual activity with strangers. Instead, society developed the convention that a polite person never spoke to strangers in the public place.

We began to walk in public space as though we were surrounded by a bubble of privacy, one (so we believed) that was protected by our silence and willingness to withdraw from public activity. If for some reason we required public conversation, we began to beg pardon for ourselves before we started. We notice this pattern today if we lose our way in a large, unfamiliar city. Only after making considerable efforts at locating ourselves do we break down and ask directions of a stranger on the street. Most people begin the conversation by tentatively saying, "Excuse me?" We hesitate to break the stranger's bubble of privacy.

Public silence became public watching. Participation in public life, the interaction with strangers, became primarily silent observation of those strangers. One need only spend some time in a shopping mall or airport to realize how prevalent this phenomenon has become. The person in the intimate society functions as a silent, passive observer when in public.

The development of the silent, passive observer in the public place is most dramatically observable in the change in the theater during the Victorian period. In pre-Victorian society an actor functioned as a servant. Members of the audience interacted freely with the actor and activities onstage and with the rest of the audience. Expressing their emotions freely with the same social conventions the actor used, the members of the audience functioned in an active, noisy, interactive manner.

As the Victorian era developed and the social conventions for expressing one's emotions in public were replaced with the psychological conditions we have been exploring, major changes in the theater took place. Now only the stage was lighted, thus visually removing the audience. Physically, the stage was raised, thus increasing the distance between stage and audience and prohibiting immediate interaction. Darkness silenced the audience, which was already obsessively worried that they might reveal themselves and shame themselves by some inappropriate revelation of personality.

In this Victorian theater, in which all but the actors became silent observers, the performer became the only person in the room who was free to express emotion. The performer began to be more important than the piece being performed. With the advent of Romanticism, which is really another name for this culture of personality, the emphasis in performance moved from the performer's skill to his or her sensibility or temperament.

The entrance of personality as the central characteristic of artistic performance is crucial for our study because it both mirrors and reinforces the psychological conditions that undergird the intimate society and influence the public nature of Christian public worship. With the dominance of personality in artistic performance, the emphasis moved from the text itself to the performer. Whether one was performing Shakespeare or Mozart, the primary interest was on the performers' expression of their personality.

In this environment, performers like Paganini, the famous Italian violinist, excelled. "One knows he is great, but not why," wrote one critic.[5] Performing became an end in itself. Paganini succeeded precisely because he made his audience forget the musical text. The entire focus was upon his personality. The audience, silent and in the dark, retreated into a passive observation of the one person who was permitted to express feelings.

It is a short step, and perhaps no step at all, to understand public worship as a reproduction of this model of public interaction. The service, now shorn of any ritual interaction that allows individuals to forget themselves in the resources of play and convention, is really a performance of one or perhaps of a small group of people who are permitted to express their true selves in public. The audience, seated in neat rows, watches the performance.

The focus is upon the personality of the performers. As the pastor climbs the stairs into the pulpit, the lights go down; everything becomes hushed silence as the performance begins. The pastor's job, like the artist's, is not to challenge and engage the audience in mutual public activity but rather to "stimulate" them.

Art, especially music in the service, becomes mere performance as well. Choirs see their mission as performing anthems and only with difficulty recognize that they are to be leaders of worship. The people in the audience are robbed of their opportunity to exercise their artistic abilities through shared activity. Instead, they sit silently observing the chosen few who are capable of public expression of deep artistic beauty. This small group often includes clergy who function as musical performers in addition to their roles as presider.

Alternatively, the more contemporary rejection of the Victorian high pulpit and the demise of the great-preaching-performance tradition continues the underlying assumptions of the intimate society. The pastor and any other performers on Sunday morning are required to expose their deepest feelings in an attempt to create the intimate community. Indeed, the higher the congregation is located on the economic scale, the more minute are the clues to the true self in worship, and the more refined the "stimulation" of the congregation by the worship leaders. Such attention to minute detail, following the Victorian pattern, is taken for sophistication.

Today's congregation may reject the Victorian high-pulpit performance but shares its assumptions. Personality rules over theology and action. Worship is in the hands of those privileged few who can act in public. The rest remain as observers.

Steven Simpler, religion editor for the *Arizona Republic,* recently described worship at the "fastest-growing Lutheran church in the Western United States [which] serves as a model for Lutheran congregations nationwide in outreach and ministry." The people "dress casually and applaud the choir and choral ensemble's performance." The pastor's sermon is in "an easy listening format." He speaks with a "conversational style of preaching and a winsome personality" that "makes you feel like you've known him all your life." He reads no biblical text as the basis for the day's topic, "How Should I Manage Stress?"[6]

Superimposition of Public and Private Imagery

In our contemporary period, we have retained the assumptions of the Victorian era in many critical instances, including the psychological conditions of involuntary disclosure of character, defense through with-drawal, and silence and the sociopsychological dynamic of fear of being shamed. The final psychological dynamic of the intimate society is the superimposition of public and private imagery, which shows up in the way we imagine, plan, practice, and experience public worship. We project private imagery upon our public worship leaders. Preachers are effective if they are vulnerable and winsome personalities. They need to act as if they and the audience have always been intimates.

The Ideology of Intimacy

The congregation projects private images onto its public life. They believe healthy congregations are like warm, open, trusting families. They debate over the personality of the congregation, as if it were healthy to have only one. They are disturbed by multiple personalities, which may be unhealthy for individuals but surely are expected of complex public communities. It is precisely this projection of the private onto the public that excludes so many strangers, both inside and outside.

Join the five psychological conditions discussed above and one has the ideology of intimacy. Such an ideology has three tenets. First, it posits that an enduring, profound human relationship of closeness and warmth is the most—or even the only—valuable experience that life affords. Second, the ideology supposes that we can achieve such an intimate, meaningful relationship only through our own personal effort and will. Third, it assumes that the purpose of human life is the fullest development of one's individual personality, which can take place only within such intimate relationships.[7] This ideology of intimacy distorts contemporary understanding and evaluation of Christian public worship.

What lessons can be learned by a congregation that takes seriously this analysis of the social and psychological dynamics of what most people, especially inside and outside strangers, experience in public worship? First, this social and psychological analysis explains the objections most Americans have to liturgical worship. They are unconsciously caught in these social and psychological dynamics. They see liturgical worship as cold, formal, and distant. It can represent to them the power classes of a predemocratic time.

When viewed from the ideology of intimacy, liturgy is, at best, nostalgically pretty; at worst, it is meaningless, since it does not enhance intimate relations or self-actualization. Its focus on public ritual seems exactly what we do not want or need. It frustrates our custom of watching a gifted few express their true selves in public. It often forces us out of our private bubble when it expects us to interact with strangers.

In light of these social and psychological dynamics, Robert Schuller's new reformation around self-esteem is not surprising. Individuals obsessed with fear of being shamed, of having their true selves involuntarily revealed in public, who are hiding in silent, sophisticated withdrawal, indeed need self-esteem. Schuller's ministry perceives the truth and responds effectively to this perceived surface need.[8]

Second, by explaining these dynamics, our analysis in this chapter gives clues for developing our strategy for welcoming the stranger in public worship. Since this is the topic of much of the rest of this book, here I only need note that any strategy for uniting faithful Christian public worship and effective evangelism must take these dynamics into account. Although we do not need to remake public Christian worship in the image of the ideology of intimacy, we do need to respond effectively to these genuine needs and perceived standards of meaningful human interaction. Those who ignore these dynamics out of blind faithfulness to Christian liturgical tradition will find themselves in a smaller and smaller elite clique who have failed as miserably as the church-growth crowd to diagnose the depths of their own response to the situation as it really is.

Third, our analysis presses the congregation to examine worship practice in light of these dynamics and the ideology of intimacy and leads to further questions regarding the driving forces behind these dynamics and ideology. Once the congregation has recognized these dynamics in their own congregational life, it must delve deeper to understand the undercurrents responsible for these surface currents.

On the basis of these five social and psychological dynamics, we could generate some principles of planning, practicing, and evaluating worship in relationship to evangelism. Such principles could be called the laws of church growth. When I read church-growth materials and observe growing congregations, I see that they are, either intentionally or not, using these principles.

Since congregations that construct worship according to these laws of church growth more often than not bring in larger numbers for worship, it is tempting to construct new worship in accord with them. Before doing so, we need to examine the driving forces beneath these laws of church growth. As real as these social and psychological dynamics are, they are only the surface currents of contemporary life. Without examining their undercurrents, a church could enjoy short-term growth but not develop worship and evangelism for sustained growth in mission. Since it is our intent to integrate worship and evangelism strategically, for the long term, we need to look deeper to discover the undercurrents of the intimate society.

2

Undercurrents
of Individualism

What drives the ideology of intimacy described in chapter 1, with its five social and psychological dynamics, is an individualism elucidated by sociologist Robert Bellah in his book *Habits of the Heart*. In both of its forms—utilitarian individualism and expressive individualism—this ideology assumes that the public space is either empty of meaning and value or profoundly less significant than private space. Both forms of individualism assume the individual is the primary reality and society is a secondary, derived, and artificial order. This view Robert Bellah and his colleagues call ontological individualism.[1]

The utilitarian individualist "takes as given certain basic human appetites and fears . . . and sees human life as an effort by individuals to maximize their self-interest relative to these given ends. Utilitarian individualism views society as arising from a contract that individuals enter into only in order to advance their self-interest."[2] The utilitarian individualist enters the public space of worship for practical reasons only: to achieve his or her desires.

Expressive individualism arose in opposition to utilitarian individualism. An expressive individualist holds that "each individual has a unique core of feeling and intuition that should unfold or be expressed if individuality is to be realized. . . . Under certain conditions, the expressive individualist may find it possible through intuitive feeling to 'merge' with other persons, with nature, or with the cosmos as a whole."[3] The expressive individualist denies the value of impersonal interaction, and thus of the public space itself, and seeks to substitute warm, intimate relationships in its place. Generally speaking, expressive individualists enter the public space of worship to experience intuitive merger with other expressive selves.

The utilitarian individualist views religion, at best, as well-meaning moral instruction. At worst, it is a private, irrational crutch for weak and sentimental people. This individualist sees the public place as a harsh, but necessary, place where people interact to achieve their private interests. They wish to protect those goals in the private sphere from intrusion of the cold reality of the public sphere.

For the utilitarian individualist, faith, religion, and the church are private business. Indeed, they are best left to "the little woman" and children, according to one physician with whom I spoke while visiting his wife and children, who were members of the parish. "I am a man of science, not given to such superstitions," said the doctor. "Mind you, I appreciate the good things you have done for my wife during her illness. You've helped her cope with this crisis and given her a sense of security. And your effect on our son is on the whole quite good. He is an insecure boy. He'll outgrow the religious myth and retain the moral instruction." This physician is hardly alone in his views.

The expressive individualist also assumes that public space has no intrinsic value. Such a person enters this space, however, to express his or her true self or to watch others who are more gifted at self-disclosure. Whenever possible, the expressive individualist organizes a community of like-minded persons to project their warm, open, and trusting private space upon the empty, cold, and dangerous public space.

In the spring of 1989, I consulted with a congregation in a relatively new suburb of a major metropolitan area. For six years the congregation had remained the same size, approximately 125–50 average worship attendance, after experiencing rapid growth in its first two years. Recently, the church was having budgetary problems and wanted to grow.

When I visited, a member of the church council, who had read a magazine article I wrote on public worship and the stranger for a denominational magazine, took me to task. She was particularly upset by my comment that growing congregations are friendly but not family in their public worship. "Why would I want to belong to a cold, public, city church?" the council member asked. "If I wanted to belong to such a church, I would have stayed in the city and belonged to one of the institutional churches. I want to feel like I am at home when I am at church so that I feel free to say what I really feel. I want others to feel the same way."

For Christian worship to be valuable for such a person, it must promote a sense of intimacy—it must be family worship. Many others share this expressive individualism. Often congregations have an extended family at the center of their activities. Members within this inner circle function as family for one another: they know one another on a first-name basis, share intimate struggles, and support one another much in the way traditional extended families do. Such relationships can be very necessary and healthy.

Effective and growing congregations do have significant relational groups.[4] Such groups focus on community building, not committee work. New groups that form reflect the interests and needs of new people. Above all, these relational groups may help the church to discover that people are more important than programs.

The ideology of intimacy is powerful even in these church circles, however, and it can exclude as well as embrace. The extended family can become a small clique that establishes the norms for worship; its needs and interests become the focus of worship. For the inner circle, worship therefore seems very warm, open, and intimate. To other members, it appears exclusive.

The pain of being excluded is particularly deep for the "inside strangers," those members of the congregation who are not a part of the extended family but who may be longtime members. Some of them may have at one time been members of the inner circle but, for one reason or another, left the core, and now when they come to worship, they have an acute understanding of what they are missing. Other members—indeed, perhaps those who most desperately need intimate support—were never invited or never joined; they may suffer the shame of not being thought good enough to be included.

If these inside strangers complain about the worship, they are tagged sticks-in-the-mud, jealous, unhappy quitters, or general troublemakers. Their complaints about the intimacy of the service, however, are valid. Whatever their motivation, they call this inner circle, often made up of the stalwarts of the congregation, to employ their strength in service of the entire community rather than of just their extended family. These strangers call the family to open its private religious world to the public world, to both inside and outside strangers.

As valuable as relational-group ministry is in the congregation, it cannot substitute for dynamic, public worship. Nor can it establish the standards by which we plan, practice, and evaluate public worship. Yet the council member who chose her congregation over a cold, institutional church was precisely about the task of establishing a law of private worship. Her attitude, shared by others, was the critical reason why the congregation was not growing.

The physician—the utilitarian individualist who relegated religion, a public concern, to the private sphere—was male. The church council member—the expressive individualist who wanted to project the private into public worship—was female. Whether these gender identifications were coincidence, stereotypes, or in fact a reflection of real differences between many, if not most, men and women has been the subject of popular and academic discussion.

In her fascinating study *The Feminization of American Culture,* feminist historian Ann Douglas documents this same division between the worlds and values of men and those of women and children and considers its effects on culture. In this study of popular literature written between 1820 and 1875, the Victorian era, Douglas exposes the origins of modern mass culture, and particularly the American conception of the feminine. She identifies popular writers by "their debased religiosity, their sentimental peddling of Christian belief for its nostalgic value."[5] In her history, Douglas traces the disappearance of theological discussion in public discourse, and its replacement with sentimental religious fiction.

A survey of the religion section in any popular bookstore verifies that this development has not slowed. More often than not, religious best-sellers pander to sentimentality through fictional nostalgia. This trend is especially noticeable on the New Age shelves in mass-distribution bookstores, where appealingly personal volumes reduce major religious traditions such as Confucianism, Buddhism, Hinduism, and Christianity to trivial generalities.

Even the detractors of the New Age may display the same contempt for religious thought. In the summer of 1989, Johnny Carson interviewed Shirley MacLaine for three segments of "The Tonight Show." He treated her as an expert in religions of the world, at the same time displaying an ironic, male superiority toward not only MacLaine but also religion. For Carson, religious experience is curious, entertaining, and humorous.

The public image of religion portrayed by both MacLaine and Carson results, according to Douglas, from the change in religious expression following the "disestablishment of clerics and women" and the exchange of roles between ministers and mothers. In short, religion has become women's business, and it has secured woman's place in the private and domestic domain all the more. The public, rational world belongs to men, and religion is not welcome there.

Both the physician and the church council member would have had their presuppositions about religion confirmed by the Carson-MacLaine conversation. The church council member would have been moved by MacLaine's sincere concern for important religious and moral questions and her willingness to learn from other people's religious experiences. The surgeon would have shared Johnny's ironic humor and sense of intellectual superiority. The conversation on "The Tonight Show" only reaffirms the utilitarian individualist's conclusion that religion is a matter for silly bimbos, who may be great entertainers but at bottom are only intellectually weak persons who need this sentimental stuff.

Oddly enough, the physician and the church council member, as well as Carson and MacLaine, agreed with one another about their faith in individualism and their understanding of the relationship between faith and reason, the private and the public dimensions of our lives.

Once, after I had spoken to a group of four hundred conservative Christians, a well-dressed man walked to the front, insistent on expressing his anger to me. He was particularly upset that I did not think Genesis 1 described the creation being completed in six twenty-four-hour days. I asked him what he did for a living. He replied that he had his Ph.D. in geological engineering and worked on the Iron Range in northern Minnesota. I asked him if he assumed, in his everyday work, that the earth was less than six thousand years old. He answered, "No, that's what I pay you to do."

Although this engineer's distinction between science and faith, between facts and values, is more obvious and simplistic than most, he expresses the common expectation of the utilitarian individualist. He is a practical man. He must enter the public work world, where God is not a part, much less an underlying assumption, of his daily life. He must bring home the bacon.

As a pastor, I represent for him the private, faith world. It is my duty to believe what he cannot. His worldview is shaped by what Wayne Booth calls the modern dogma.[6] He believes that reality is separated into two distinct spheres: the world of "scientific" facts and the world of irrational, subjective "Christian" values. In his Monday-through-Saturday world, he does not doubt what the so-called scientific facts are. He cannot do so and function as a geological engineer. Yet, according to his Sunday world, the world of values, the world ought to be less than six thousand years old. So he lives in this fact-value split. The facts are what are; the values are what ought to be.

The distinction between what is and what ought to be, between fact and value, is at the heart of the modern dogma. Although this distinction has not won total acceptance in the academic community, in the last seventy-five years or so, the imaginative universe of most educated Western people has increasingly been divided into facts and values. Karl Popper, one of the clearest defenders of the split, summarizes the view this way: "It is impossible to derive a sentence stating a norm or a decision from a sentence stating a fact; this is only another way of saying that it is impossible to derive norms or decisions or proposals from facts."[7] For proponents of the separation, facts never lead to value judgments; an "is" can never become an "ought," no matter how long you stare at it. Reality, according to this commonly held belief system, is divided unequally: there are a very small number of indubitable facts and a very large number of absolutely unprovable values.

Facts are the products of reason and observation. They are a part of our outside world and are available to all reasonable persons, regardless of race, gender, or class. They are public.

Values are irrational. They come from an individual's emotions and prejudices. If they are shared at all, they are shared with intimates. They are within, private, and do not belong in public.

In educated circles, this modern dogma has fostered a raging debate between those Booth calls scientismics, and those he labels irrationalists. The scientismic understands facts as important contributions to knowledge and values as unimportant. He or she might divide and evaluate knowledge, as in Table 1.[8]

The irrationalist, the person who accepts the fact-value split but believes that values are important, would characterize these same things, as in Table 2.

We could continue these lists indefinitely. The utilitarian individualist often takes the scientismic view, believing that public life can and should be lived on the basis of facts alone. The expressive individualist reacts strongly to utilitarian individualism and the scientismic view. He or she often takes the irrationalist view, believing that public life is, at best, the opportunity to express a genuine self and, at worst, a cold, reductionist world one ought to avoid. The debate between these two sides will continue as long as both sides accept the modern dogma, since the debate between the scientismist and irrationalist makes sense only if one accepts the sharp split between facts and values.

Table 1: Scientismic View

Good	Bad
known facts	asserted values
objectivity	subjectivity
reason	faith, prejudice
science	opinion and rationalization
proof	assertion, emotion, rhetoric, propaganda
neutral universe	invented values
empiricism	idealism

Table 2: Irrationalist View

Good	Bad
values	mere facts
persons, subjects	things
faith, commitment	cold reason
mind, spirit, the soul, personhood	materialism
wisdom, real knowledge	scientism
the significant, knowledge of the heart	the provable
the self, the soul	human reduced to machine
holism	reductionism

The separation of fact and value, according to this modern dogma, leads to the separation of public from private. Public and private life are two exclusively separate realms, best kept apart at all points. The public is the place of reason, which, according to the scientismic, speaks with a universal voice. In the scientismic perspective, one imagines a separation between "public minds" and "private desires."[9] Some proponents of this position have firmly believed that reason and passion can be completely divided and that, since "reason speaks in one voice," our public lives should be governed only by this supposed universal reason.[10]

Religion, according to this perspective, is clearly a private matter, since it is not derived from facts but depends upon irrational desires. If we are to govern ourselves rationally, religion, the sum of our irrational desires and prejudices, must be excluded from the public sphere. Religion should concern the private sphere of family, women, and children.

When I call this dogma "modern," I do not mean it is only a generation or two old. In part, its profound influence stems from its central place in the understanding of the Founding Fathers. Thomas Jefferson, who was reticent to speak about his private life, was especially reluctant to reveal his religious beliefs. He was convinced that religion was essentially a private affair between each person and that person's God. He even refrained from religious discussions with family members, as one of Jefferson's grandsons, who was very close to him, testified.

> Of his peculiar religious opinions, his family knows no more than the world. If asked by one of them his opinion on any religious subject, his uniform reply was, that it was a subject that each was bound to study assiduously for himself, unbiased by the opinions of others—it's a matter solely of conscience; after thorough investigation, they were responsible for the righteousness, but not the rightfulness of their opinions; that the expression of his opinion might influence theirs, and he would not give it![11]

Christians have not taken Jefferson's position completely to heart. We do provide for the education of our children in the Christian faith, but aside from a few exceptions, we keep that education located in the appropriate private spaces of home and Sunday morning. In fact, the acceptance of this modern dogma by different church bodies can be traced to the Victorian period, when most Protestant religions began to accept Sunday school as the primary location of Christian education and to reject the value of parochial schools or the teaching of religion in public schools.

In popular Christian theology, this acceptance of the modern dogma leads to an image of God who has two faces: one face of God is public, and the other is private. At worst, we claim that there are in effect two Gods: the public god, God the Creator; and the private god, Jesus the Redeemer.

Often the public god, reduced to "Nature's god"—in whom, every American coin reminds us, we trust—has been identified with God the Father—the benign, distant, even absent Providence. It was to this god that most of our politicians invited our prayer. This god creates and preserves us. This god is exceedingly abstract and distant, a perfect fit into the scientismic, mechanical image of the universe.

By contrast, the private god is the Jesus who is in our hearts or the Jesus in whose heart we find relief. This private god is the intimate, warm one. This god "walks with me and talks with me, and tells me I am his own." This god is our personal savior. Unfortunately, these two gods seem to have little to do with one another, leaving many mainline Christians forced to serve two gods, one public and one private in the somewhat schizophrenic fashion that the geological engineer chose.

The modern dogma also creates a false division in another area crucial for public worship: art and artistic expression. According to the modern dogma, art is a matter of taste and to that extent is irrational and private. The irrationalist side of the modern dogma rejoices in this relegation of art to the private and the subjective. For the irrationalist, art can then become the expression of the individual artist. It does not need to be publicly available, nor does it serve public purposes. Some irrationalists even believe that purposeful art would be degraded and would fail to be true art if it entered the public sphere. Others, while not giving up their irrationalist perspective, believe art ought to be the public expression of the emotions and private opinions of the common people. This belief commonly leads to a form of public artistic expression "geared to" the lowest common denominator.

In the church, relegating art to the private or to the taste of small groups of connoisseurs or turning it into a lowest-common-denominator expression of individual emotions defeats the possibility of worship that is open and welcoming. It also leads to unfortunate struggles over the use of art in public worship.

The pastor, who is often ill prepared to integrate music effectively into public worship, may be intimidated by competent church musicians. If he or she accepts the judgment of the modern dogma that music is a private, irrational matter, he or she may conclude, "I don't know anything about music, but I know what I like." If the pastor exercises final judgments and does not like what the church musician likes, the battle ensues. On the other side, the church musician often develops an intimate clique who share the same taste in music. This small group, perhaps a section of the choir, establishes its own private agenda for "beautifying" the worship, but it has little sense of the role of music in public ritual.

Many similar possibilities for conflict flow from placing art and music within the private sphere, under the influence of the modern dogma.

That should not be surprising in our society, where art is not understood as an essential human activity but as the province of a few gifted persons. In the world of the modern dogma, the aesthetics of the performance becomes the focus of worship. The technical excellence of a few, and not the publicness of the service, becomes the criterion of success.

Even if church musicians are inclusive, calling upon others who are not the designated artists to deliver a selection or to join in at the chorus, they do not thereby make worship public. Rather, church art simply becomes the helter-skelter expression of the members' momentary feelings, a private worship in a public place.

The modern dogma divides more than Sunday from Monday, men from women and children, god from god, art from public life; I could add many other illustrations. In general, however, we have seen that because of the modern dogma, faith, religion, and the church are experienced as private, fueling the self-consciousness most individuals feel during worship. We are encouraged to think of our congregations as families and to welcome strangers with the demand that they too become members of the family.

Before turning to my proposal for welcoming the stranger in public worship, it will be instructive to review the attempts of faithful Christians, through the liturgical renewal movement, to reconstruct public worship in the face of these contemporary currents and undercurrents.

3

Undercurrents
and Liturgical Renewal

Good liturgical worship and effective evangelism belong together, despite the commonsense idea that they are incompatible. This common sense arises out of our experience of liturgical worship in the intimate society and is driven by the modern undercurrents, which I have called the ideology of intimacy and individualism and the modern dogma, all of which affect Christian public worship on two levels: how we experience it, and how we think about it.

These undercurrents may result in vastly different perceptions of public worship. The scientismist will experience public worship as a set of empty, irrational motions rising from the most primitive instincts of a prehistoric humanity. In contrast, the irrationalist experiences (or at least expects) public worship to be home, where the intimate community realizes the identity of the individual and the collective through individual self-expression. The scientismist expects little from public worship, and the irrationalist expects much; indeed, he or she expects precisely that experience against which public worship stands as an alternative. Thus, both the scientismist and the irrationalist are bound to be disappointed by public worship, no matter how it is tailored to meet their expectations.

At the strategic level of theory about public worship, these modern undercurrents profoundly affect our ability to reflect on, and to discuss with one another, the nature of our worship experience and the manner in which we wish to develop it. If religion, religious experience, and ritual are private and irrational value systems, they are also matters of public ignorance, for most people can hardly talk intelligently about them. Ignorance about our own religious experience and reticence to discuss it in public are the order of the day. The more formal education irrationalists have, the less knowledge they seem to have about religious experience and expression; the culturally sophisticated function as religious adolescents, at best.

Nowhere is this childishness more evident than in the area of liturgy. Many Christian ministers, and even more parishioners, are woefully ignorant about the liturgy. Their theological knowledge is modest; their understanding of the anthropological, sociological, and psychological functions of liturgy is nonexistent.

Liturgy is most likely of all the theological disciplines to be placed squarely within the category of values by the modern dogma. For both the scientismist and the irrationalist, liturgical concerns are just matters of taste. They are not really central to human experience or reflective of divine reality, according to the scientismist. Or they are romantic reflections of a unified world represented by the divine mystery in worship, or a nostalgic repristination of the fourth or the fifteenth centuries, for the irrationalist. But both agree on one thing: to each his own; the importance and effects of liturgy are not subject to public conversation.

Too much liturgical scholarship has taken this most unhelpful route charted by the modern dogma. The teaching of worship, especially in most Protestant seminaries, is lodged in the practical department, where it runs the risk of being reduced only to helpful hints or techniques. If we are to avoid reduction of the rituals of public worship to a matter of personal taste or practical techniques, we must make major changes in how we think about worship. If the scientismist and irrationalist are to have different experiences of public worship, the practice of worship must change.

Liturgical Renewal Fights Back

Although the need for major changes in public worship may seem overwhelming, we also have the gift of abundant resources for response, some of them already in place. Over the past two hundred years, as these modern undercurrents have developed and driven our public life, the church has not been wholly acquiescent to their demands upon popular culture and the academy. In many ways, the church has effectively challenged these undercurrents with respect to Christian public worship, with the most significant response being the liturgical renewal movement beginning in the late nineteenth century.

This renewal movement, which transcended denominational boundaries, refused to accept the destruction of public worship by the modern dogma. When others were prepared to abandon Christian liturgy as an irrational primitive or a hindrance to free self-expression, the liturgical renewers struggled to restore the vibrance of Christian liturgy and its central place in the life of the church. This chapter traces the heroic efforts of the renewers, who, motivated by pastoral concern and faithfulness to Christian tradition, strove to sustain the life of Christian public worship, even though they themselves were infected by the modern undercurrents.

The liturgical renewal movement came in two major waves, the first originating in the nineteenth century with liturgical reforms on the European continent and separate movements at Oxford and Cambridge. Various sources are linked to this first wave. In France the first wave is linked to Prosper Gueranger (1805–1875) who refounded the Benedictine priory of Solesmes on July 11, 1833 and set into motion "the world-wide liturgical movement that has reshaped the worship of many branches of Christendom."[1] In England, within days of the events in Solesmes, John Keble (1792–1866) preached a sermon that lead to the Oxford Movement. The Oxford Movement, following the impetus of Keble, and the leadership of J. H. Newman (1801–1890) and E. B. Pusey (1800–1882), "transformed the established Church of England and eventually the member churches of the Anglican Communion."[2] In Germany, the first wave of the liturgical renewal movement is traced to the German Roman Catholic theologian Johann Adam Moehler[3] and the various liturgical revisions brought about by the influence of the Prussian Union of the Protestant churches.[4]

Much of this Protestant renewal was restorationist in character and explicitly over and against attempts to erase differences among confessional traditions. In Germany, the work of Theodor Klieforth (1810–1895), Ludwig Schoeberlein (1813–1881), and Wilhelm Loehe (1808–1872) brought about profound changes in German Lutheranism both in Germany and the United States, especially in Indiana, Michigan, and Iowa.[5] In Denmark, Nikolai F. S. Grundtvig recovered liturgical traditions and brought about a revival of hymnody.[6]

The second wave is often traced to a speech given in 1909 by Belgian Benedictine monk Lambert Beaudin, the first of many Benedictines who later joined pastors and academics of other traditions to produce this second wave of renewal.[7] Beaudin's work is reflected in the work of the American Benedictine Virgil Michel and the British author A. G. Hebert. They also show up in the work of Gregory Dix, who is the culmination of "a great series of English liturgical scholars."[8] In Germanic circles Josef A. Jungmann, S. J., was of great influence. His conservative and careful "portrait of the history of the mass shows how important a tool historical studies can be in pastoral efforts."[9] All of these and others profoundly influenced the second wave of liturgical renewal best exemplified by the work of Vatican II in the *Constitution on the Sacred Liturgy.*

Both waves have profoundly affected contemporary worship patterns in the vast majority of Christian congregations in western Europe, Canada, and the United States.[10] Indeed, both of the movements rejected the scientismic perception of Christian liturgy and, primarily through historical research, defended the reality and public sense of Christian liturgy to the general public and academia. "Before," what the social historian Robert W. Franklin calls "the disdainful frowns and sneers of liberal, secularist skeptics who looked upon churches and religion as more or less archaic hangovers from the past, destined, like warfare, to fade away in the light of reason and self-interest,"[11] these movements proved the enduring value and power of Christian ritual to modernity.

In addition to the scientismist (liberal, secularist skeptics), these movements also took on some of the more destructive social realities resulting from industrialization. The nineteenth-century movement was "marked by its effort to teach women and men to find in prayer a meaningful activity with social implications in the midst of economic hardship."[12] Liturgical renewers set up house in the midst of the most hard-hit urban communities and joined their efforts at liturgical renewal with the restoration of civil and economic community. Whatever the relative success of these attempts, they were characteristic of the nineteenth-century movement and give lie to the claim that it was solely motivated by the aesthetic interests of a privileged, intellectual and economic elite.

Within the church, they combined historical research with appeals to Western mysticism, in hopes of renewing Christian liturgy. They sought to find the genius of medieval and ancient church liturgical tradition, to reach back in time and behind the texts to the power of ritual as an "elemental form of discourse."[13] Within the church, they combined historical research with appeals to Western mysticism, in hopes of renewing Christian liturgy.

In the sections that follow, I first sketch the two major liturgical renewal currents in the twentieth century that resulted from these waves and then briefly describe a third, but less significant, renewal current. Next, I describe the effect of the modern dogma upon these currents, and finally note the surface eddies that flow from these currents as they have blended with the hidden undercurrent of the modern dogma. Finally, I summarize what I characterize as the unfinished business of the liturgical renewal movement: its failure to be hospitable to the stranger.

Three Currents in Liturgical Renewal

My mentor and former colleague Henry E. Horn has described three currents on the surface of liturgical renewal, each of them driven by the undercurrents of modern life.[14] For easy understanding of these currents, imagine that the twentieth-century liturgical renewal movement is a vibrant stream of water and, furthermore, that we put some dye into the water to trace its currents. The first current, marked by red dye, begins in the early nineteenth century and carries into the first half of the twentieth century. The second, or green, current begins in the first decade of the twentieth century and continues to the present. The third, or yellow, current is the folk worship revival of the 1960s, which died more or less quietly in the early seventies but which in very important ways represents an excellent example of how an apparently counter-cultural liturgical movement can be profoundly influenced by the modern dogma and the intimate society.

The red current of the liturgical renewal movement, which began in Europe, faced a great challenge in restoring physical rituals to American Christian worship practice because of increasing division among American Catholics about the appropriate ritual for the new culture. Mid-nineteenth-century Protestants met an even more difficult situation, for they had little, if any, organic tradition readily available. In order to restore physical ritual, to integrate mind and body, public and private, they chose to retrieve the most available and perhaps to them the most authentic liturgy available—the late fifteenth-century medieval worship.

Subsequent liturgical renewals in this century, which I have named the green and the yellow currents, similarly retrieved previous liturgical practices that were not organically continuous with the contemporary experience. While all three movements were necessary and very valuable

attempts, foundational arguments that the reformers made in support
of retrieving particular worship patterns often took on a romantic tone.
As one liturgical scholar put it in a session introducing the *Lutheran
Book of Worship,* a product of the green liturgical renewal movement,
"One must choose one's century. It is time Lutherans stopped making
the sixteenth century their norm and chose the fourth! That is what
the *LBW* does." As will be clear from a discussion of these currents,
that romantic tone is only one evidence of the significant role that the
modern undercurrents continued to play in the worship of the church.

The Red Current

The first liturgical renewal current of the twentieth century grew out
of the revived historical consciousness in nineteenth-century Europe.
During the 1840s, with the Oxford and Cambridge movements, this
renewed historical vision fastened on the late Middle Ages as a sort of
idyllic time for Christianity.[15] In the view of the renewers, during the
Middle Ages the church was integrated with culture; this was truly the
time of Christendom.

Their choice of a liturgy formed in an era of a secure Christendom
helped these early nineteenth-century renewers project a safe Christian
sense of public worship upon what they perceived to be a dangerous,
empty public space. By restoring its liturgy, they thought, they could
restore the past, at least in those fleeting moments of worship.

Those in the Cambridge movement turned toward a recovery of
Gothic church buildings, establishing authorities whose sole mission
was to authenticate architectural details, vestments, ecclesiastical arts,
and paraments. In fact, the leaders of the Cambridge movement went
out of their way to emphasize that they were not interested in theological
dispute. Rather, they claimed, using scientismic sorts of arguments, they
were simply following good empirical research models in their study of
medieval church architecture. As one who recognizes the fact-value split
might predict, the Cambridge movement was attacked first from without
and then from within by those who questioned these claims of objec-
tivity, pointing out that even the authoritative authentication of architectural detail was dependent upon certain aesthetic and theological
values.

However valid the criticism of its methodology, the Cambridge movement and those that followed it must be credited with turning the
church's attention to the importance of liturgy and liturgical space. By

reviving a concern for liturgical architecture, these first renewers rein-troduced a sense of holy space in public worship.[16]

In Catholic circles, J. A. Moehler, the Tübingen theologian and student of Schleiermacher, began a liturgical renewal that, though it was conceived in the rarified atmosphere of the theological seminar, soon took shape in parish and monastic practice. He questioned from a distinctly Catholic perspective certain suppositions of post-Napoleanic Prussian culture. "If there will be no higher power than the state in Europe, then human freedom has come to an end," he argued in 1837.[17] In contrast to rising nationalism, he offered a Christian vision of "a free, international religious community, the Catholic Church," within which "individual liberties . . . could be guaranteed."[18]

Within this free, international religious community, he developed a thick description of a renewed social community. Central to this renewed social community was the restoration of social mission and liturgy. His students at Tübingen took his ideas into parishes and communities and stimulated a profound social movement and revival in German Ca-tholicism.

A major force toward German liturgical recovery was the king of Prussia, Friedrich Wilhelm III, who produced a liturgy for his newly united church.[19] The king's reform was heavily influenced by a desire to restore an "ideal" liturgy. His reforms are responsible for reawakening liturgical interest within Lutheranism.

Equally significant for American liturgical reform among Lutherans was the work of Wilhelm Loehe. He joined together mission and li-turgical renewal. His liturgical scholarship reflected a reaction to the wordy public worship of the previous century and its lack of missionary commitment.[20]

Though the work of liturgical renewers like Loehe was significant in Germany, their most profound effect was upon the various mission fields to which graduates of the mission academy went. Among these mission fields were several communities in the United States formed by ever-increasing numbers of immigrants arriving from central and southern Europe.

Although Moehler and the French revival at Solesmes had profound influence in Europe, more influence than Loehe had on Protestant Germany, it can be safely said that they also profoundly influenced Catholic American worship patterns and liturgical scholarship. Perhaps the most noted example of direct influence is St. John's Abbey, the German Benedictine community in Collegeville, Minnesota where social mission and liturgical reform became the central focus of community. From places like St. John's Abbey, many parishes were invited into liturgical renewal, and as a result of liturgical scholarship at places like St. John's, the church at large, through the liturgical reforms of Vatican II, affirmed major changes in the parish practice of the liturgy of the church.[21]

In general, whether Catholic or Protestant, the immigrants of the latter part of the nineteenth century and the early part of this century, who were affected by the liturgical renewal movement, brought with them a liturgical practice foreign and, in many cases, unacceptable to their neighbors. Catholic liturgy was identified with tradition and papal power; Lutheran worship, with ethnic and class ignorance; and Anglo-Catholics were said to be class snobs. Whatever the reasons, the immigrants felt considerable pressure from their neighbors to give up their liturgical heritage, one that was in part a product of liturgical renewal in Europe.[22]

In fairness to their neighbors' point of view, their worship practices did appear out of continuity with reigning American practice. It looked medieval and smelled of privilege to imaginations formed in the modern dogma and the intimate society. It was frightening at a profound level, since it struck at the very undercurrents we have uncovered in the first two chapters.

They appeared medieval, of course, because the primary resource for red-current restoration was the medieval liturgy on the eve of the Reformation. These sixteenth-century sources were used in a fairly legalistic manner by those in authority. In simplified form, we may characterize the red current as follows:

1. The rubrics, or general directions, were all-important. The object was one standard liturgy that was protected by rubrics saying when one *shall* or *may* act in certain ways. The *shall*s protected the integrity of the liturgy; the *may*s allowed for some freedom and experimentation. Many clergy were always confused, however, and stuck to the *shall*s.
2. There was always clerical leadership in this movement. The laity had only responsive parts in liturgy.
3. The emphasis was on sacred space.
4. Because late-medieval worship had a strong individualistic bent, it fit neatly into the focus of the modern period, with its focus on the individual. The result for corporate worship was the gathering of individuals who more or less worshiped alone in a public setting.
5. Finally, it was generally assumed in the red movement that worship took place within the idea of Christendom. It was assumed that worship was

public, that it was aimed at the whole community rather than the faithful alone.

The psychological conditions characteristic of the intimate society in its Victorian period are clearly present in the assumptions of the red current. The worship audience consists of individuals who have defensively retreated into a passive silence in public worship. Their passivity accentuates an already-existing clericalism and ultimately feeds, as fire is hot, anticlericalism.

In mainline Protestant circles, liturgical renewal within the red current was shaped by attempts to restore respectability to a tradition reacting against the revivalism of the nineteenth century. Revivalism, whose tenets were completely in accord with the modern dogma, understood religion, religious experience, and worship to be primarily irrational, private matters. The revival movement sought to move the religious affections in individuals so that they would have appropriate emotional religious experiences.

Dignified, middle-class Protestants in this century, particularly in the period between 1920 and 1945, according to James F. White, reacted against the vulgarity of revivalism and its exaggerated manifestations of religious experience. They did not, however, give up the underlying assumption of the modern dogma that religious experience was essentially a private matter. Rather, these renewers simply placed the emotions of revivalism into gentler, more tasteful categories of aestheticism.[23]

Public worship during the aesthetic period was no less directed by the modern undercurrents than was its predecessor, although its chief concern was not expression but elegance. By contrast to vulgar expressions of religious anxiety and fervor in the nineteenth century, symbolized by the public-worship tradition of the anxious bench, the aesthetics expressed themselves in muted tones, particularly in response to a sophisticated preaching performance from a high pulpit. In the aesthetic reforms, the music and vestments of worship became more refined, and the sentimental character of Christian worship inherited from the nineteenth century was made only more respectable.

The Green Current

The green current, the second great liturgical renewal movement in the twentieth century, also has its roots in nineteenth-century scholarship. This one emerged from four basic changes in the world of theology and liturgical thought following the First World War. These changes intensified in the 1930s and 1940s.

The first theological change responsible for the green current was the breakthrough in biblical studies. Since the turn of the century, biblical studies have been more and more ecumenical.[24] Especially following Pius XII's encyclical "Divino Afflante Spiritu" (1943), the efforts of Catholic biblical scholars have increased, and they have joined arms with Protestant and, to some extent, Orthodox scholars.

The impact of this ecumenical biblical scholarship on liturgical renewal is multifaceted. First, it puts scholars from traditionally antiliturgical churches into contact with contemporary Catholicism, a meeting that has eroded many unfounded anti-Catholic prejudices. Much of the historical retrieval has also led to a growing appreciation of Christian liturgy as the Christianization of Israel's worship.

Second, ecumenical work has brought insight from the Far East, which has affected liturgical renewal as well. In South India, for example, many denominations were portraying their divisions before Asian converts who did not care about European denominational clashes. The churches tried to bring their traditions into sensible harmony for these neophytes through a new approach to liturgy, by choosing the early church Eucharist as a model. The result is the liturgy of the Church of South India, an influential force in green-current Protestant liturgical studies.[25]

The place of patristic studies in the ecumenical liturgical renewal cannot be ignored. Perhaps most significant in this development is the work of Gregory Dix. In his book *The Shape of the Liturgy,* Dix set the tone for the liturgical use of patristic scholarship. One passage, in particular, captures the rather romantic turn that this use of patristic scholarship took. Dix described the early fourth-century liturgy in terms of a Victorian gathering in a wealthy middle-class home. Although he explicitly tried to avoid sentimentalizing the age, the patently romantic tone of these passages did as much as anything else to shape the liturgical renewal of the green current.[26]

A third element responsible for the green current is the worker-priest movement. Before and after World War II, the Catholic church of France realized that it had missed contact with the working class. A number of younger priests offered to give themselves, at subsistence pay, to live among other workers, say mass at their factories, and carry on a mission to them where they lived and worked. Thus started about ten years of heroic work.

This effort did not go as planned, however; the workers could not make the cultural jump that the mass demanded, and as a result, they did not attend. Instead, the priests, through their concern for the worker's lives, made common cause with their grievances and became their vocal advocates, often joining the Communists in their protests. The priests' associations embarrassed the established church, and worker-priest efforts were terminated. But this effort to relate work and worship had a profound effect on congregations nearby, and it tied social action to a renewal of eucharistic action.[27]

Finally, a momentous change had come upon the consciousness of European Christians and their mission outposts around the world. The nineteenth century produced missionary enthusiasm that counted the whole world as territory for the expansion of the Christian church. That zeal stirred up so much enthusiasm that at the turn of the twentieth century a journal renamed itself the *Christian Century.*

Two world wars and the accompanying disillusionment with Western culture, however, together with the completely unexpected reappearance of world religions in force, led to reevaluation of the idea of a worldwide Christendom, a melding of Christ and culture. In place of the Christian century, a very different world evolved, one in which Christians were in the minority and probably would always be so.

The idea of Christians as a permanent minority and the loss of missionary zeal profoundly affected the conception of Christian worship. The emphasis moved from the melding of Christ and culture to accepting significant discontinuities between them. Sunday morning, no longer Christendom at worship, became a small, highly intentional community of the faithful, the people of God. The liturgy became less a public act and more a peculiar act of this small but faithful few. This is overdrawing the distinction for the purposes of exposition; the contrast is clearly present, however, if one compares books such as *Service Book and Worship* and *Lutheran Book of Worship; The Book of Common Prayer* (1928) with *The Book of Common Prayer* (1979); and *Methodist Hymnal* (1965) with the new *The United Methodist Hymnal* (1989).

The result of these four factors—biblical studies, ecumenical work, the worker-priest movement, and consciousness of being a minority—on the liturgical practice of the church is the green current, which in the United States built up in the 1950s and early sixties. We can characterize as follows the green current as it was adopted in the United States:

1. The green movement refocuses concern upon the image of the church as the people of God.

2. The movement emphasizes a self-consciousness of one's called, baptized state as bringing one into this people.
3. The activity of the laity in worship in leadership and actions is greatly increased, even emphasized.
4. Worship, then, has a more corporate conception. Worship is thought of as what the people of God do in God's presence.
5. Holy people replace sacred space as the major focus of worship.
6. Nonverbal, symbolic language comes into worship and includes gestures and visible signs.

The psychological conditions of the intimate society, now in the more contemporary form, are present in this green current as well. When the church is understood using the imagery of the people of God, or even the family of God, an important shift has taken place. It is very easy for the gathered community to think of its space as precisely private space.

Gregory Dix's analogy between a church and a small Victorian home where a small number of the faithful gather pictures well the modern dogma's relegation of religion to the private. Once the premises of private space are accepted, the focus upon the church as the people of God, or the family of God, can easily take on the character of the congregation as the collective personality. The tension between all people as the people of God and the church as the people of God is lost.

The characteristics of the green current do not necessarily aid and abet the intimate society. These same characteristics, if construed differently, can counteract the forces of the intimate society and provide the basis for a readjusted liturgical renewal, which we consider in the following chapters. Rather than imagining public worship as the gathering of a persecuted minority in a safe, private home, we can imagine these same liturgical resources within a public space where strangers are no longer either anomalous or suspect.

The Yellow Current

Unlike the green current, which had pervasive effects on liturgy, the yellow current affected the church primarily through its youth ministries; it also was common in campus ministry. Songs produced using secular tunes popular with youth were used not to replace liturgical chants but to give a bored younger generation some incentive to join worship.

As a teenager in the late 1960s, I was attracted to the liturgical renewal that was at the center of both Catholic and some Protestant youth groups in my hometown. It was only natural that when I attended university, I would become active in the experimental liturgies common on that campus in the late sixties and early seventies.

The experimental mood of this liturgical renewal was timed perfectly for the results of the Second Vatican Council. During this time, Catholic parishes were moving from the Latin Mass to a more dialogic and congregationally oriented vernacular service. At least in several parishes I know, the youth liturgical renewal became its own ecumenical bridge in many Catholic parishes. The Catholics during this time provided what Henry Horn calls "a folk-mass avalanche." To me, it was more like riding the crest of a wave.

What I could not see then, but what is clear now, is that the youth movement was really a new Pietism. It majored in small-group psychology and methods. The guitar, an intimate, small-group instrument, became all-pervasive. When it was amplified with a leader at the mike, it imposed a new dictatorship of liturgical action. Small-group singing accompanied the guitar. The texts identified with the oppressed over against the establishment. We were the intimate community over against the cold public space.

The yellow current was certainly opposed to the red current, which had bored its young worshipers to death and failed to produce an intimate and safe space. The focus upon selfhood (which is probably natural for adolescents) became an obsession. Not only adolescents but their parents as well were inundated with "youth-identity-crisis" literature, and almost everything in youth ministry was ruled by this focus on self.

The relationship between the yellow and the green currents is more complicated, for both are essentially small-group movements aimed at recovering the early church. It is no accident that campus ministries were the sites of experimentation by both the folk advocates and the experimenters with green-current material.

For better or worse, the youth liturgical movement has been swallowed up by time. Nothing passes faster than nostalgia, especially when it is nostalgia for a time and place the nostalgic never experienced and that, in the eye of the critical historian, probably never existed. The yellow current was more like a child's ideal of the people of God than a ritual practice that could sustain the public worship of the church. The youth liturgical renewal, for all its strength, only intensified the privatization and sentimentalization of public worship.

In their attempts to retrieve an earlier moment in the life of the church, all of these liturgical currents are drawn along by the undercurrent of the intimate society. They differ, of course, in the century they choose and the way they construe the basic ingredients of public worship. As I will suggest, however, they share basic commonalities that we explore before I turn to the eddies that their differences create.

The most evident of these eddies results from the meeting of the red and green currents and manifests itself most immediately in the problem of worship orientation: where is the focus of attention to God's presence during worship—toward the East, or toward each other as God's people? Second, these eddies ask what attitudes we should adopt in gathering in God's presence: an attitude of awe and mystery, or an attitude of familiarity, of the everydayness of meeting the people of God in God's presence? Third, the eddies question whether Christians should take a predominantly verbal approach to worship or one that emphasizes ritual action and nonverbal expressions. Fourth, they raise the question whether laypersons or clergy should lead worship. Fifth, they ask whether confirmation is a critical rite of passage to first communion or simply an affirmation of our baptisms.

Most American parishes are caught "betwixt and between" the red and green currents. The red current, with its retrieval of late-medieval worship, focuses on the presence of God spatially to the East, to the altar, and, because of their location, to the clergy. Congregations worshiping in buildings designed for this Eastern construal of the presence of God are confused when they try to follow the rubrics (a habit fostered by the red current) using a green-current liturgy. Because the green current attempts to retrieve the ideal of the fourth century, with its focus on the people of God as a small but highly intentional group gathered in a home, the style of the congregation must change substantially to follow those rubrics. Confusion and conflict are a common result.

Commonalities in the Currents

Even the surface eddies that result from the meeting of these three currents illustrate the effect of the modern undercurrents on liturgical renewal in the intimate society. The liturgical renewers tried to infuse into congregational life the traditions of various centuries, but they have not attended adequately to the new context. They have thus rediscovered tradition, but they have not recovered it. Instead of discovering a new religious experience that is related to the first liturgies but more appropriate for their present situation, renewers have handed the contemporary church a series of choices with few theological, anthropological, and sociopsychological means of evaluating those choices.

In understanding the process of retrieval primarily as analysis of past liturgical texts to recover the genius of the original text and the situation,[28] critical scholarship fails to focus on the constructive moment in the present. In this usually irrationalist model of retrieval, history is the lived experience of the faithful, and the evil to be conquered is the dominance of dogma over history. The much-used Latin tag *lex orandi, lex credendi* (literally, law of praying, law of believing) has become the battle cry for this romantic retrieval. The law of prayer, understood as the genius of a past golden age recovered through historical research, should rule the law of believing. A romanticized past, in the hands of a few with influence and authority, is thus handed down as obligation to congregations caught in these eddies. Ironically, these careful scholars have missed the grammatical ambiguity in the Latin when they translated the tag into English. Rather than suggesting that the law of praying determines the law of believing, the Latin phrase underlines the reciprocity of relationship between the two laws.

Like liturgical theologian Geoffrey Wainwright, who has uncovered this ambiguity,[29] I see the ambiguity as a happy one because it emphasizes precisely what has not been attended to in any of the liturgical renewal movements: theological reflection and religious experience must be held together within the public category of law. The red current has seen the importance of the law of prayer in its concern for rubrics, but ultimately it followed the path of rubricism and respectability so typical of Victorian culture. The Oxford movement, for example, developed a complex set of rules for the placement of a myriad of liturgical accoutrements. As a scholarly movement, it presented itself similarly as an even more refined and detailed historical account of previous liturgical practice.

Conversely, while green-current scholarship has rejected the rubricism of the red, it has almost exclusively focused on historical studies for determining its critical, public activity. Rather than refocusing its attention on the present, the green current has merely taken the third and fourth centuries in exchange for the red current's romanticization of medieval Christendom at worship.

Indeed, the fact that one document—*Apostolic Tradition,* written around A.D. 215 by Hippolytus, bishop of Rome—is the resource for a major portion of the green current illustrates how contemporary liturgical renewers are tempted to romanticize a single time and place. James F. White notes how it is difficult to decide whether Hippolytus should be considered a third-century or a twentieth-century liturgical renewer, since his influence on the twentieth is for all practical purposes much greater than it was on the third.[30]

Whether the late fifteenth or the third and fourth centuries provided their norm, these two liturgical renewal movements placed the bulk of their critical analysis on the accurate reproduction of a historical moment. Their decision to make the historical into the primary critical moment has damaged opportunities for local ownership of liturgical renewal and caused unnecessary conflict within the church. The reality that the renewers were disproportionately monks and other male religious, many of them academics, has only added to the cynicism of laypeople, who may understand the renewal as something handed down from above or good only for mystics.

In the period from 1945 to the present, "a liturgical establishment has developed" from these renewers' movements. While this liturgical establishment has generally served the cause of lively Christian public worship, the movement itself has not been particularly hospitable to the stranger. According to James F. White, himself a member of the establishment, "We must also question how representative the establishment has been. Increasingly an effort has been made to include blacks, hispanics, women, and youth on worship commissions. But too often these people have remained silent during discussion or not appeared for meetings."[31] White recognizes the necessity of including those strangers whom I have called the obvious, or outside, strangers. Surely any renewal of Christian public worship that wishes to take seriously hospitality to the stranger as a central principle of worship will include the outside strangers. It is, however, one thing to recognize that need to be hospitable, another to accomplish it.

Similarly, the liturgical renewal has not done well with those who are not directly related to the liturgical establishment. Hospitality to the stranger as a central principle of liturgical renewal would deliberately seek out those who are alienated and take seriously their experience.[32]

The disregard for contemporary experience and the limited scope of the intended participants in liturgical renewal have been exacerbated by the almost total focus upon historical retrieval. While the recovery of our liturgical heritage was necessary following the Enlightenment, many of the renewers did not adequately distinguish between tradition, "the living faith of the dead," and traditionalism, the "dead faith of the living."[33]

Traditionalism obscured the critical force of the gospel to which Jesus calls us and which he embodies. The life, creativity, and sense of local indigenous worship in response to God's presence too often were discouraged by the liturgical renewers. By doing so, they largely avoided any critical analysis of modern and contemporary sociopsychological currents and did very little critical theology that was not a history of ideas. However strange it may seem that pastors of the church should ignore these currents, examination of the entire project of liturgical renewal in light of the two modern undercurrents—individualism and the modern dogma—clarifies how they have blinded even well-intentioned and educated renewers to the demands of the contemporary situation.

A Dialectical Proposal

The three major liturgical renewal currents (red, green, and yellow) have been unconsciously affected by the modern undercurrents. These movements, in their reaction to the scientismic-rationalist view of worship, reveled in ritual and tradition. Liturgical scholars of the first two movements (the only two that most serious liturgical scholarship considers) focused their critical energies on the historical retrieval of the intentions and experience of the original congregation, after a choice of century. The demands of contemporary culture as it affects worship practice and theological application were relegated to secondary status in the public conversation.

Even today, critical use of theological principles in the development of liturgical practice is rare. Although detailed examination of contemporary anthropological ritual studies or sociopsychological and cultural studies is being used more, they are often poorly integrated with theological and historical studies. In short, the main battle line in both academically based liturgical movements in this century has been drawn between history and dogma, with no small amount of animosity against dogma and critical theology.

If historical analysis is the only critical moment, however, renewers will inevitably succumb to the temptation to impose upon the contemporary church a romanticized historical description of a past liturgical practice. As I have suggested, the most popular example—the phrase *lex orandi, lex credendi*—can easily fall prey to this pattern. Liturgical scholars are properly interested in history, especially the history of prayer and of liturgical renewal activities. But evocation of the principle *lex orandi, lex credendi* requires a deeper understanding of the complex relationship between liturgy and theology than is often the case among the liturgical renewers, at the levels of both practice and theory.

In contrast to this either-or logic of history versus dogma, I call liturgical renewers to recognize the dialectical relationship between systematic theology and historical theology, consistent with Johannes-Baptist Metz's observation that "the fundamental hermeneutical problem today is not how systematic theology stands in relation to historical theology, how dogma stands in relation to history, but what is the relation between theory and practice."[34] Unfortunately, the insistence in all three liturgical renewal movements on relegating worship to the private, irrational categories of taste and sentiment all but guarantees that Metz's question will not be confronted. Instead, new liturgies will continue to be handed down from above, from people who have done the appropriate historical scholarship, people who are said to have good taste. Without a theological argument for this liturgy, worship copied from the rites of some idyllic golden age of the church will inevitably be severely discontinuous with the experience of the people, both in the pews and outside them.

If my analysis regarding the effect of the modern dogma on these liturgical movements is accurate, two major changes need to be made. First, a more critical dialogue between history and dogma, along with contemporary critical theology, needs to take place. Second, a major effort of liturgical scholarship should be placed upon the dialectic occurring between theory and practice. Such a refocusing of energy would take into account in an integrated manner the particular context of the worshiping community and would see critical theology, dogma, anthropology, and sociology as ancillary disciplines to liturgical scholarship.

On the parish level, this same shift of emphasis would lead to the development of local theology and worship that, while remaining faithful to the tradition, would feel far less obliged to some universal ideal of the liturgy handed down from some higher committee. This change in emphasis would commit parish clergy to ensure that the teaching of ritual competence and theological critique takes its proper place in the education and practice of pastors and other ministers of the church.

In summary, while they brought new vigor to the church's worship, the liturgical renewal movements of this century have been diseased by the modern undercurrents, which prevent the church from ensuring the health of its own public worship or aiding in the establishment of a viable public life outside the church. I suggest, however, that there is a needed place for liturgical renewal and that the critique I have made of the renewers' efforts in this century can be overcome with positive proposals consistent with many of the concerns of the green current for continued liturgical renewal and committed to effective evangelism.

4

The Stranger
and the
Self-Giving God

Although the experience Barbara Whiterabbit and I shared in the nave
of the church was profoundly driven by contemporary undercurrents,
it has parallels in Scripture and the early church, which faced the same
challenges of a world in turmoil as diverse cultures confronted one
another. The historical period immediately before the life and death of
Jesus and the birth of the infant church was a time of religious pluralism,
though not freedom of religion. During the six hundred years of Hellenistic culture following the death of Alexander the Great (in 323 B.C.),
no single religion enjoyed the public status that Christianity would
occupy after the Roman emperors Constantine and Licinius recognized
Christianity as one, but not the only, religion of the empire (in A.D.
313). In Hellenistic culture, many religions and philosophies vied for
adherents in the public world.

In addition to the significant parallels between biblical times and our
present experience, the Scriptures provide the horizon within which to
develop a contemporary public theology of worship and evangelism.[1]
The public ritual of the biblical tradition was, in many respects, more
foreign to most of the early Christian converts than our Western Christian public ritual is to the average newcomer to worship. The realities
of racism, classism, and sexism, although perhaps not as conscious a
challenge then, nonetheless challenged the biblical tradition of worship.
These same elements that characterize our experience also shaped the
early church's struggle to make public its witness to the gospel. Barbara
Whiterabbit and I were thus simply repeating a common scene in the
biblical tradition.

Just as the metaphor of hospitality to the stranger best expresses how we should respond to the contemporary dilemma we face, the theme of hospitality to the stranger forms "a major substratum in the New Testament," according to John Koenig.[2] Its prevalence in Scripture attests to the importance of the public, evangelical dimension of worship in the biblical tradition and reveals how public ritual embodied this central theological and moral concern. Indeed, this metaphor of hospitality to the stranger bridged the two worlds of every worshiper's life, opening one's private dimension to the church through the church's public rites.

This chapter first describes how Israel remembered itself as the stranger whom God graciously hosted. The New Testament presents this image of God's self-giving, self-sacrificing presence in Jesus' meal fellowship, interpreted through his fate and ministry. The theological principles that ground this pervasive theme of reserving a place for the stranger, particularly in worship, are two. First, God is the host of public worship, whose presence is often revealed in and through the stranger. Second, the God who is present in worship is essentially a gracious God who gives to the stranger.

We extend this theme by exploring the tension between early residential churches, where hospitality to the stranger was centered on table fellowship, and the work of itinerant missionaries, who depended on more-established residential churches, generous hosts, and synagogues. The dynamics of these centers of hospitality is always centrifugal, outward in mission.

By the end of the Hellenistic period, this mission strategy took shape as what church scholar Robert Webber calls liturgical evangelism, "a conversion experience regulated and ordered by the liturgical rites of the church."[3] Liturgical evangelism, described at the end of this chapter, was the church's response to the pluralism it encountered, the bridge between the private and the public dimensions of catechumens' lives.

At each of these stages in the development of a ritual of hospitality, Christians understood their rituals of fellowship as rituals of liberation. In the meal fellowship, in church hospitality, in liturgical evangelism, as in the church's contemporary Eucharist, God is acting to liberate the Christian community to trust in God's promise, a trust that frees them to live always as hosts and members of a company of strangers. Ritual space and time are transformed by this image of guests gathered by a gracious host; worshipers enter an odd space and time to form an extraordinary community where ordinary social relationships do not apply. In the ritual of the table, guests may respond to the presence of the self-giving God, and explore and revise their public and private worlds.

Provision of hospitality to the stranger is full of dynamic conflict. It requires a decentering of our self-centered lives that is most disturbing. It requires risk and wisdom, since the stranger can and does do us harm. It means that we must be prepared to have the tables turned, to discover that we are the guests in need of hospitality. Above all, it requires that we not only recognize but also appreciate that reality is plural and that we cannot simply force it into the strictures of the intimate worlds we have created. Rather, the other must remain in important ways "other," different. Hospitality to the stranger, as we will see in the biblical witness, requires the transformation of the self in such a radical manner that this transformation often is referred to as repentance and conversion.

Israel's Worship and the Stranger

The importance of the stranger to Christian worship reflects the strong continuity between Christian worship, especially during the life of Jesus and in the early church, and the worship of Israel; we may say that Christian worship is the Christianization of Israel's worship. We can understand the biblical witness to Christian public worship and the stranger only by attending to Israel's understanding of the place of the stranger in public worship.

Over a period of 1,500 years, no matter where the people of Israel were located, their worship was focused on the stranger; indeed, the prophets were critical of Israel whenever it failed to reserve a place for the stranger. Concern for the stranger is a necessary, though not sufficient, condition for public worship, according to this tradition.

From its nomadic period onward, Israel remembered that God's will was revealed for Abraham and Sarah when they were hospitable to three mysterious visitors (Gen. 18:1-21). Israel's captivity in Eygpt was described in the image of the stranger as well: "When an alien [RSV: stranger] resides with you in your land, you shall not oppress the alien. The alien who resides with you shall be to you as the citizen among you; you shall love the alien as yourself, for you were aliens in the land of Egypt: I am the LORD your God" (Lev. 19:33-34).

Israel's status as stranger reminded the people that in public worship, Israel was the guest of the Lord. Public worship was primally God's act, the ritual hospitality of the Lord extended to Israel as beloved and honored guest. Israel was also reminded, however, that in the events of the exodus, God chose Israel over the existing Egyptian social structures, creating a new community. Since Israel was the recipient of the Lord's hospitality, so Israel's worship was to be hospitable to strangers. As God is host to Israel, so Israel is called to be host to the stranger.

The image of God as host in public worship is underlined by the description of the tabernacle, and then of the temple, as "the Lord's house." David is not allowed to build a temple, since the building of this new house waits on the Lord's command. When Solomon's temple is finished, his prayer of dedication at the same time recognizes the presence of the true God and implores God to hear and respond to the foreigner's petitions. "Likewise when a foreigner, who is not of your people Israel, comes . . . and prays toward this house, then hear in heaven your dwelling place, and do according to all that the foreigner calls to you . . . that they may know that your name has been invoked on this house that I have built" (1 Kings 8:41-43).

The reserved place for the stranger and the public character of worship both depend upon God's presence. Though God was free to be present everywhere, God promised to be present in Israel's worship. Through this promise, God initiated Israel's worship. God's presence authorized and necessitated the presence of the stranger, and thus Israel's worship was essentially public.

God's presence established the logic of public ritual. The liturgy was thus an expression not of how Israel saw things but of how God saw Israel and all people.[4] Liturgy was not, then, a human device to hold God on reserve but a gift from God of God's self. This presence was available to those whom God invited. Since God invited the stranger and was known to come as the stranger, the stranger could not be excluded.

God's presence as stranger was not always the same. According to the Old Testament scholar Terence Fretheim, God's presence in ancient Israel took different "intensifications," and the language used to describe God's presence reflects these gradations of presence. Between God's general presence in creation to God's theophanic, explicit presence was God's "tabernacling presence (the choice of a specific place to dwell among his people)."[5]

In focusing on public worship as the tabernacling presence of God, we recognize an essential trait: Israel's gracious God was self-giving. Such a trait is important for several reasons. First, it emphasizes that

God is gracious, giving not only things that belong to God (the earth and its abundance) but also God's very self. Second, the expression "self-giving God" emphasizes that God gives of God's self continually, in God's ongoing action in the world. God seeks to communicate and to give God's self, not only in the past, but also now, in the present, and in the next moment.

Thinking of God as self-giving helps us to avoid some of the liturgical pitfalls that the more traditional language of grace creates. If God's gift of self-presence is understood as substance, it is easy to imagine God presenting grace wrapped in a box—the liturgy—with our job to pry the box open in order to get the gift. Once the box and the object have become separated, it is easy to focus our attention either on the box or on the object. Those who reject ritual believe they can throw away the box (liturgy) in which the gift comes and concentrate solely on the gift. By contrast, those who value ritual tend to focus too much of their attention on the box; they worry too much about getting the ritual right, and worship becomes mechanistic. In either case, the basic ritual logic of the self-giving God is lost.[6]

The emphasis on God as host in ritual, as giving of God's self, reminds us that grace is indeed a relationship that is initiated by God's promise and sustained in its fulfillment of the promise. If believers are conscious of the liturgy, they have missed the presence of God. Ritual behavior works precisely because it draws attention away from the self and allows people an opportunity to greet God.

To presume that there can be an immediate relationship with God, however, without such "outward" things as ritual, is simply to ignore the logic of giving oneself. According to liturgical scholar James White, if we are to understand the critical role of ritual as creating Christian public worship, we must understand the three conditions for the giving of self: a self that is capable of giving, a recipient, and a means of giving.[7]

An important part of an infant's early development is precisely learning how to give of itself. Only if a child has been the object of such giving can it develop a sense of self that can give itself to others. The interaction of parent and child shapes a self in the child, who can eventually give of itself. Similarly, God as host, as giver, must appear for us to learn how to host the stranger.

Without a recipient, however, the giving of the self is not possible. Even if persons are not immediately present, they must exist for us to give ourselves. Abstract self-giving that has no particular individuals as its object, such as presumed self-giving to the church, is not giving at all. Similarly, one does not love in the abstract; one requires a person to love. Without the other, our worship is similarly lifeless.

Finally, the means of giving ourselves are words and actions.[8] Through words, we "speak our mind" to others, giving up our privacy and inviting others to share in our thoughts. When we refuse to speak, we close ourselves off from the other. We saw in chapter 1 how public life in the intimate society is often characterized by strangers passing each other silently, refusing to share even the slightest bit of themselves through a casual greeting. By refusing such ritual greetings in the contemporary public space, we refuse to give of ourselves even to the extent of acknowledging the value of the stranger's presence. Although we may indeed value the presence of strangers, the silence of our tongues and gestures powerfully expresses our fear in their presence.

In the biblical tradition of public worship, God prompts self-giving in three ways. The worshipers spoke *to* God, they spoke *for* God, and they spoke *to each other* in God's name. The psalms were often the expression of worshipers speaking to God, although their speech to God grew out of God's promises. Thus, the psalms grew out of God's prior speaking, and the psalmist responded out of the full range of human experience. Through the reading of Scriptures and their interpretation, the worshipers spoke on God's behalf. Through words of greetings and comfort, for example, the worshipers spoke words to each other in God's name.

We give ourselves through actions as well as words. I can give myself to my family by daily housekeeping. The most extreme example of giving myself is giving my life for another. Housekeeping and dying for others are part of a complex spectrum of actions, often joined with words, that allow us to give ourselves to one another. Actions like shaking hands, especially with strangers, are rituals that make possible the giving of our selves to others.

Ritual actions in the temple, home, and synagogue were the means of receiving God's gift of self and of the worshiper's responding to that presence. Worship, then, was a combination of God's activity and what the worshipers did when they were conscious of God's presence. By its complexity, the ritual served to exclude, as well as include, the stranger; the logic of the ritual, however, was essentially designed to gather in the stranger.

God's promise to be present in Israel's worship was commonly abused. The temptation Israel faced in constructing its ritual was to localize God's presence in the temple and domesticate it. In such domestication, the temple became God's only home. Israel could claim to have God in a box, so to speak, and to control the development of an intimate, secure, and warm relationship.

Although this domestic temptation was powerful, Israel guarded against it through a variety of spatial images. For example, the transcendent imagery of God's home in heaven (see Ps. 11:4) and the cherubim-throne (1 Kings 8:6-7) in the temple reminded Israel that God was not limited to this address but could "fly" (Ps. 18:9-10). The ark was deposited with its carrying poles intact (1 Kings 8:7-8). The Holy of Holies, dark and inaccessible, underlined the transcendence of the divine presence.[9] One of the strongest reforming traditions to correct these attempts at domestication, however, was the ritual concern for the stranger.

The prophets are often falsely portrayed as rejecting the public ritual of the temple, in favor of a more spiritual relationship between God and Israel. In support of this portrayal, passages like Hosea 6:6 are cited: "For I desire steadfast love and not sacrifice, the knowledge of God rather than burnt offerings."

In fact, the prophets often were tied to the public cult, a pattern that they shared with other Near Eastern cultures. The beginnings of prophecy in ancient Israel were tied to the cultic center (1 Sam. 9:13; 1 Kings 14:2; 2 Kings 2:1, 3). Later, priests and prophets served together in the temple (Jer. 23:11; 26:7; 35:4; Lam. 2:20). Much of the prophetic material reflects liturgical settings; Psalms, for example, contain prophetic oracles (Pss. 50, 81, 82, 95).

Rather than being anticult, the prophets often criticized temple ritual precisely because it excluded those whom God would include—the stranger, the marginal, the poor, and the widow. Though it is clearly lodged against certain worship practices, this criticism calls into question not the practice of the cult per se but its relationship to issues of justice. Obedience to these requirements of justice and repentance with respect to our failure to attend to the stranger are central to true worship and acceptable ritual. The importance of the stranger to ritual and, hence, the importance of this public character of ritual are therefore strengthened, not lessened, by the prophetic criticism of Israel's ritual practice. In the stranger, God could be unexpectedly present under all circumstances, and proper ritual included the space reserved for the stranger.

Christianizing Israel's Worship

The earliest Christian communities were made up mostly of Jewish Christians, who brought with them a significant heritage of public worship. Jews of the first century worshiped in three settings: the temple, the home (especially around the dinner table), and the synagogue.[10] Each of these settings contributed to the shape of public worship and the place of the stranger within it.

The Temple

The temple in Jerusalem at the time of Jesus and Paul was a very public place; strangers were engaged through a common set of actions. It was an important public place for the Jewish nation, as well as the Diaspora (those Jews who were spread throughout the world) and the general population of Palestine, which included many non-Jews. The ritual activities of the temple structured much of the public life of the city of Jerusalem. From all indications, Solomon's prayer on behalf of the foreigner was put to the test regularly, though only certain parts of the temple were accessible to the gentile.

The life and ministry of Jesus, especially in Luke, is at several points connected to the temple. In its Holy of Holies, John the Baptist's birth is announced to Zechariah (Luke 1:523). As an infant, Jesus takes part in the temple rites of purification (2:22-24). On this visit to the temple, he is recognized by two strangers (Simeon and Anna), who reveal his purpose and destiny (vv. 25-38). In this temple, during the annual Passover visit by his parents and kin, he engages in the public activity of teaching and learning among the temple officials (vv. 41-50), to whom he describes the temple as "my Father's house."

In Luke-Acts early Christians are described attending worship at the temple (Luke 24:53; Acts 2:46; 3:1-10), and Paul, in his final visit to Jerusalem, enters the temple (Acts 21:26-36). Important parts of the New Testament, especially Paul's letters, reflect a time before the destruction of the temple (ca. A.D. 70) when the temple was perceived as an appropriate place of worship for Christians. This Jewish Christianity brought with it important traditions from the temple worship, not the least of which was its public character.[11]

The temple is also the object of criticism by early Christians. Stephen attacks the temple cult as a purely human institution founded by Solomon (Acts 7:47-50). Stephen believes that the corruption of Israel's worship is yet one more factor that led up to and includes the killing of the "Righteous One," Jesus. The Gospels all record that Jesus will cleanse the temple, and each predicts its destruction. For example, in Mark's Gospel, Jesus foretells the destruction of the temple (13:2) and is accused of claiming, "I will destroy this temple that is made with hands, and in three days I will build another, not made with hands" (14:58). This ironic accusation proves to be true: through Jesus' death, the temple is destroyed (in the Gospel, symbolized by the tearing of the temple curtain), and through his resurrection, a new temple, the church, is created.[12]

One central theological claim made by attacks upon the temple cult is that in Jesus the need for the temple's sacrificial rites has ended. Such critics argue that in Jesus' sacrificial death, temple worship has been superseded by the presence of the One who was sacrificed.

Yet, the temple provides the image within which the work of Jesus as the Christ could be understood. Paul made this point, even before the temple was destroyed, when he writes that God has put forth Christ as a "sacrifice of atonement [or place of atonement] by his blood" (Rom. 3:25). Paul declares him an atoning sacrifice (alluding to the ceremonies of the Day of Atonement, Leviticus 16) and writes further, "Our paschal lamb, Christ, has been sacrificed" (1 Cor. 5:7).[13] Just as Christ replaces the sacrificial ritual of the temple, the church is the continuation of the temple, now not one made with hands. Similarly, the use of psalms in Christian worship is strong evidence of the continuing influence of the public form of worship characteristic of the temple.

The Home

In the emerging Christian communities of the New Testament, the residential churches are the primary site of public worship. The ritual traditions surrounding the meal in the home included a reserved place for the stranger. Hospitality to the stranger remained an inherent part of worship in the home and remained, in this important sense, a public event.

Residential churches developed from a Jewish tradition: even before the destruction of the temple, Jews regularly worshiped at home. For instance, the Passover ritual was set in a home, in keeping with the events of Israel's liberation from slavery that the ritual represented. These events served as the historical precedent for the ritual mediation of God's presence. Ritual in the home was not restricted to the Passover meal. Each meal was accompanied by its own ritual, indicating its divine source and sacred purpose. The Sabbath meal in particular was ritually celebrated.

From the worship setting of the home meal radiates much of Jesus' ministry. He is often described as a guest at someone's table, and many of his most memorable parables are told during and around a meal. Indeed, his eating and drinking with sinners particularly offends the good and righteous. Most important, in the meal Jesus underlines the inclusive nature of the realm of God, which he often compared to a monarch's feast.

The themes of abundance and hospitality characterize these mealtime parables. Although Jesus and his disciples engaged in no sustained wage-earning labor and had given up regular family life, they seemed to enjoy the hospitality of many, both poor and rich. The abundance of their food and drink depended not upon their industry but upon the generosity, thankfulness, and hospitality of their hosts.

In *New Testament Hospitality,* John Koenig argues that this theme of abundance and hospitality, characteristic of Jesus' life and ministry, is the way to understand the realm of God. Jesus was calling people to a change of mind and heart in keeping with the coming of God's realm. The change, often called repentance, moved them from isolation to "the fullness of community life which God had always intended for Israel." As a result, the abundance of God was "offered in Jesus' ministry through the central metaphor of a banquet."[14]

God is the host at this banquet; he gives far more than people need or deserve (Matt. 5:43-48). Out of this lavish giving comes the sinners' repentance and the power to leave behind their isolation and join the community life that God intends for all. Repentance here follows God's giving rather than preceding it; it is clearly not the condition of God's prodigious giving but a possible result.

Such extravagant giving poses a shocking contrast to our self-centered hoarding. Although the giving of God may bring remorse and shame, it is intended to relieve preoccupation with the self. The worshiper enters into table fellowship through the ritual structures of the meal. These rituals allow one's self-consciousness to recede and the presence of God for and through the stranger to dominate. God's generosity creates a response of thanksgiving and a willingness to share this abundance. Those who see and believe are opened up to a public life of generosity and hospitality to the stranger. Those who do not believe see only scarcity and are lost in their own hoarding.

The community of disciples gathered around Jesus reiterates this message. They came from various socioeconomic strata, though perhaps not from the very rich. John Koenig imagines that "Jesus and his disciples must have confused their Galilean contemporaries," since they were so diverse and depended so heavily upon "the giving and receiving of welcomes."[15] Tax collectors and fishermen were not usual companions, and given the subsequent conflicts among them, they were not "one big happy family." To the contrary, they might best be described in Parker Palmer's phrase, as "the company of strangers." They needed to learn and relearn hospitality to the stranger, not only to expand their company, but to maintain it.

Jesus' company of strangers was in this sense a public community that depended upon God's giving and, out of gratitude, shared God's abundance through hospitality to the stranger. Elisabeth Schüssler Fiorenza argues that the group gathered around Jesus was nonpatriarchal in structure and included women as disciples. Such an inclusion of women would only demonstrate how radical was Jesus' view of his company and of God's inclusive abundance.[16] The power of God's abundance opens to all individuals life in this company of strangers. If Schüssler Fiorenza is correct, this is a public life that includes women.

God's abundant giving takes its most extreme form in Jesus' giving of himself. God's giving includes self-sacrifice. On the night he was betrayed, Jesus thus took bread and wine and gave himself to the company of strangers who were his disciples. He linked these actions and words regarding his fate and ministry to the breaking in of God's realm. In this meal, through his self-giving, self-sacrificing presence, their lives were opened up to and through the stranger.[17]

Luke develops this "through-the-stranger" theme extensively. Jesus is the stranger born in the stable. In Luke's description of Jesus at banquets, Jesus always enters the scene as one who needs hospitality. As the banquet proceeds, however, the role of guest and host, stranger and known, are reversed. For instance, in the home of Simon the Pharisee, Jesus is at first the guest. Jesus then takes charge, however, by telling a story and announcing God's forgiveness to the woman who has anointed his feet. The guest (Jesus) is through the stranger (the woman) revealed as the ultimate host.

Numerous biblical examples illustrate this role reversal, by which Jesus as the stranger opens the door to the realm of God and welcomes the other.[18] Perhaps the most memorable is the scene on the road to Emmaus on Easter Sunday evening. A stranger joins two of Jesus' disciples who are engaged in conversation regarding the most recent events in Jesus' life. This stranger appears to be the only person in Jerusalem not to have heard of these events. As they walk, the stranger begins to unfold for them the Law and the Prophets and shows them the connections with Jesus' fate and ministry. As they reach their home, the stranger begins walking on, but the disciples offer him their hospitality, which he accepts. As they sit down to eat, he takes the bread and blesses it. Then he reveals himself as the Lord and disappears.

The relationship of host and guest, where the guest is a stranger, takes on an ultimate claim in the context of Easter evening. Matthew draws this claim out in his portrayal of the last judgment. Jesus appears and begins dividing the righteous from the unrighteous. To the righteous, he talks about how they clothed and fed him; to the unrighteous, he says, "I was a stranger and you did not welcome me. . . ." The unrighteous reply, "Lord, when was it that we saw you hungry or thirsty or a stranger or naked or sick or in prison, and did not take care of you?" To this Jesus replies, "Truly I tell you, just as you did not do it to one of the least of these, you did not do it to me." Matthew concludes, "And these will go away into eternal punishment, but the righteous into eternal life" (25:43-46).

Paul is equally clear about the importance of hospitality to the stranger, most importantly in the house churches that developed in the early church. Koenig characterizes Paul's development of this theme as "welcoming one another to new humanity."[19] It is central to Paul's gospel that in these social settings, Christians welcome one another as Christ had welcomed them (Rom. 15:7).

Paul grounds the evangelical mandate to welcome others to the new humanity, especially in the gathering of the church for fellowship and the Lord's Supper, in Jesus' suffering, death, and resurrection. These events are the center of God's transforming power, which makes possible our welcoming one another to new humanity.

Paul understands the Lord's Supper in particular as God's liberation for participation through Jesus' death and resurrection. In his first letter to the Corinthians, Paul's distress focuses on meals. As one might anticipate, given the size of these churches, which numbered between ten and sixty members, and their location in comfortable middle-class homes, the Corinthians have allowed their gathering for fellowship and Eucharist to become more like the meetings of a private club than a welcoming of one another into new humanity. Apparently the richer members of the community, who bring from their abundance, are eating and drinking and well into their private party before others, presumably the poor, arrive. This self-centeredness Paul condemns.[20]

Paul recognizes the diversity of gifts, talents, and socioeconomic positions among believers. He rejects these differences, however, as an excuse for turning the gathering of the house church into a private party of like-positioned persons. Rather, he insists that these diverse benefits "can be distributed, beginning in worship, so that all members receive due honor and strengthening for their particular vocations."[21] The exercise of the diverse gifts of the community simply increases the abundance from which the new humanity can live.

The conflict in Corinth is particularly instructive for our exploration of the public character of Christian worship. The tendency (perhaps natural) to privatize the meal had to be rejected because it gave lie to the central claim of the gospel, namely, that in God's self-giving, self-sacrificing presence in this meal, a new humanity—even a new cosmos—was being made. Thus, the eucharistic meal was not to begin before all were given a chance to gather. The inclusion of those on the periphery and the ordering of the community's table fellowship quite against ordinary structures of social life were essential to the gathering.

The early eucharistic ritual was critical to this hospitality. The ritual effectively insisted upon the presence of the whole community before the meal could begin. According to New Testament scholar Gerd Theissen, the order of service favored by Paul to guarantee the participation of the entire community was quite fixed. First, the whole congregation gathered, a process that could take some time. The community should not proceed, however, until all were given the chance to gather. Second, all would prepare food, which was donated by the wealthier members of the congregation. Third, Jesus' words at the last supper were repeated over the bread. Only after this liturgical repetition could the full meal begin. Finally, the eucharistic meal was ended with drinking of wine and concluding blessings.[22]

The eucharistic meal was deliberately odd, and it expressed, precisely through its ritual oddity, the entrance into an extraordinary community. This community was an alternative ordering of life, both private and public. The liturgical form was a way of creating the bridge between the private and public. This bridge made possible the free movement and witness to the gospel and protected access for the stranger and the marginalized.

The worship in the home, characteristic of Jewish worship, was carried on into Christian worship. The theme of hospitality to the stranger important in the Jewish home-worship tradition is taken up and intensified in the ministry of Jesus. Jesus is portrayed as the stranger who initially appears as needy guest but is revealed through hospitality to the stranger as the ultimate host. As such, he offers, through God's abundance, a great banquet to which all strangers are invited. To secure and realize this invitation and the coming of God's rule, God gives God's self in Jesus' suffering, death, and resurrection. In turn, those who enjoy this self-giving, self-sacrificing presence are moved to repentance and hospitality to the stranger.[23]

The Synagogue

As with house worship, the role of synagogue worship is important in understanding public worship in the church. Most of the early part of our Holy Communion service (the synaxis) comes directly from the synagogue worship. The apostles and early Christian itinerant missionaries, like Paul, often attended the synagogue, where they made their initial contacts in a city. Although the synagogue would eventually be closed to Christians and the house church would dominate Christian public worship until the time of Constantine, public worship in the synagogue shaped the biblical tradition's content as well as its mission form.

For Jews in the Diaspora and throughout Palestine, the synagogue was the chief place of worship, instruction, and community life. The rituals of the synagogue, however, were not fixed. Typically these synagogue services followed the pattern of prayer, Scripture reading, and (if a competent person was present) homily.[24] These practices were clearly public ones: not only was the tradition of the reserved place for the stranger left intact, but the preaching and reading were by their nature inherently public acts. The open discussion of Scripture readings was interactive; while it had its own ritual, such instruction also allowed for a lively interchange of opinion and interpretation.

The liveliness and openness of the synagogue setting can be readily seen in Jesus' and Paul's experiences with the synagogue. Jesus as an itinerant preacher could be invited to read the Scriptures and comment upon them. One such incident, although it ends with his rejection, illustrates the public nature of the synagogue worship (Luke 4:16-30). Jesus was in his hometown, and "as was his custom," he went to the synagogue (v. 16). As he rose to read, the book of the prophet Isaiah was handed to him. As Jesus read from the prophet the promise of the liberation of the oppressed and then sat down, with all the eyes of this company upon him, he declared, "Today this scripture has been fulfilled in your hearing" (v. 21). When the audience turned hostile, Jesus exited, as yet untouched.

Paul, too, as itinerant preacher, takes the offered opportunity to speak in the public setting of synagogue worship. At times, he provokes responses as dramatic and violent as those to Jesus' first sermon in his home congregation. Other times, he is welcomed by members of the community and invited to stay with them in their homes. Because the synagogue welcomes him publicly, Paul's itinerant mission is enhanced and others are given the chance to extend hospitality to the stranger, who proves to be the herald of the ultimate host.

In the early Christian church, the itinerant missionary typically is dependent upon the hospitality of the synagogue. Later, house churches often host these itinerant preachers, and missionaries like Paul depend upon their hospitality in order to carry out their traveling mission.

Luke, in the Acts of the Apostles, writes to encourage such a mutually hospitable relationship. Luke's emphatic discussion reflects considerable tension between the residential churches and these itinerant preachers. In many ways, his discussion of this tension best summarizes early Christianity's struggle to go public with their worship. The house churches sought a more intimate and domesticated form of Christian life, the itinerant preachers a more occasional style. Luke writes to the residential community, without denigrating the achievements of these charismatic missionaries. He encourages, according to Koenig, "a co-operative missionary effort characterized by a fluidity in guest and host roles on the part of travelers and residents alike."[25]

This dynamic relationship of host and guest allowed a diverse spiritual-material interchange. The local churches became communities gathered around the meal, and they invited their neighbors to join them. They were also the home bases for itinerant missionaries who would establish younger resident churches. Both the resident and the itinerant worshiped in public, showing hospitality to the stranger.

Early Evangelism and Worship

A chief source for our knowledge of the method and content of evangelism in the early church is Hippolytus's *Apostolic Tradition*.[26] This source must be read with a certain skepticism because it cannot represent the practice of the church in all situations and because Hippolytus was clearly arguing a particular position as *the* tradition.

Hippolytus tells us that the evangelical method of the church was really a process of bringing a person into Christ and full communion with the Christian community. The process had at its center baptism and included four distinct stages: (1) a period of inquiry, (2) a time of instruction, (3) an intense spiritual preparation for baptism, and (4) continued nurture in the church. In order that these four stages would be given public scope and recognition, they were set off by public rites of passage: the rite of entrance into the time of instruction, the rite of election into the intense period of spiritual preparation, and the rites that surround baptism. These four periods of growth and development framed by three rites of passage are the bridge upon which the private and public dimensions of conversion were brought together.

This chapter has rehearsed the biblical importance of God's hospitality to and through strangers and the church's hospitality to strangers, focusing on two forms of worship found in the biblical tradition: one centered on the table fellowship and the other on preaching and reading of the Scriptures. These two forms of worship were linked by the several stages of liturgical evangelism, the bridge giving free course to the gospel, enlivening the public life, and calling the stranger into Christ.

Contemporary public worship that is faithful to this heritage of worship will be characterized by hospitality to the stranger, especially the socially marginalized. It will mediate a purely private faith and one open to the public in an outward-directed mission—what we call evangelism—that is ever present as at least a dimension of every form of Christian public worship. As H. W. Gensichen says, "Everything the Church is and does must have a missionary *dimension*, but not everything has a missionary *intention*."[27]

Despite the temptation to make Christian worship a private act, especially with persecution and official rejection, this missionary dimension remained in the early church. The church continued to sponsor public worship, except under the most severe persecution, pursuant to several basic principles that also summarize this chapter. The first principle is that God is the host of Christian public worship, one whose self-giving presence often comes through the presence of strangers. The second principle is that God in Christ is the victor over the powers of evil. The presence of this victorious Lord liberates the Christian to live a life of hospitality to the stranger. The third principle follows from these theological principles: the church is a hospitable, nurturing, mothering community that in its nurturing remains open to the stranger. The fourth principle is particularly crucial for our considerations: external rites can be critical means of ordering internal experience, thus making possible the healthy integration of the public and private dimensions of Christian life.

5

A Gospel-Centered
Public Worship

When I was in high school and college, I was a drum major in the marching band. Early on, I learned that it was easy to see when the ranks were uneven. Indeed, anyone with eyes to see and ears to hear could find some problem with the band. It was another matter to know how to fix the problem. To make the band play and march well required an understanding of the depth of the problem: knowledge about certain personalities in the rank, the difficulty of the maneuver or music, and so forth. It also required a vision to shape and motivate specific actions and a plan to achieve specific goals.

We have similarly observed some problems among the ranks in public worship in the church in social and psychological terms and summarized them using Parker Palmer's concept of the ideology of intimacy. We described these problems as surface currents driven by two undercurrents: the modern dogma and the pervasive belief in individualism. We explored these undercurrents and their effect upon contemporary congregational life, especially worship and evangelism, and the attempts of faithful Christians to counteract the effect of these forces upon the church through the liturgical renewal movement. Our purpose in this analysis was to give us critical tools for understanding the unnecessary conflict between liturgical renewal and effective evangelism and to provide resources for developing an alternative strategy for integrating faithful and effective worship and evangelism for the present mission of the church in North America.

In chapter 4 we read the biblical tradition with these contemporary circumstances in mind and followed the biblical narrative's understanding of the relationship between public worship and hospitality to the stranger. We now turn to some specific steps that can renew contemporary public worship so that the wisdom of the liturgical renewal movement can be coupled with effective evangelism. Such a liturgical renewal must do more than reproduce a past liturgical practice. It must relate the public and the private lives of the congregation in new ways. Indeed, it must draw upon church liturgical resources as a means to enliven the church as a public community and institution in a culture of pluralism.

In this chapter, such a strategy of liturgical renewal begins by thinking theologically and theocentrically within the biblical metaphor of hospitality to the stranger.[1] The chapter imagines God, the other, the self, the church, and finally public worship and evangelism within the metaphor of hospitality to the stranger. The first sections outline a theology of public life from the perspective of hospitality to the stranger. From within this general outline of a theology of public life, the latter sections develop a theological strategy for public worship and evangelism.

These latter sections imagine that the presence of God establishes the logic of the church and, hence, public worship and evangelism. They imagine the church as an evangelical conversation and life on behalf of the world, characterized by hospitality to the stranger. Such a church bridges the public and private spheres of life, as does the liturgical renewal of public worship and the contemporary need for evangelism.

The God of Abraham and Sarah: The Stranger, the Other

In our contemporary setting, it is easy to domesticate hospitality by imagining it to be simply a way we invite a few select persons into our private space, making of them intimates. The biblical vision we explored in the last chapter, however, reveals hospitality to the stranger as far from a domesticated encounter. In the biblical narrative the threat of the stranger physically, emotionally, and spiritually is fully recognized. Indeed, when the biblical characters encounter the stranger face-to-face, they encounter not only another person who cannot be reduced, without remainder, to analogies to themselves, but they encounter the ultimate Stranger, the irreducible Other, God.

When the three strangers came off the desert, Abraham and Sarah had no idea who they were. Even when they invited them to rest and eat, Abraham and Sarah still did not know who these strangers were.

At first these strangers were black dots on the horizon of the desert; as they approached, they took on human shape, and finally they had faces. They stood before one another, face-to-face.[2]

Such face-to-face encounters are primordial to human existence as a self-conscious self. Before we exist as an "I," we exist face-to-face as strangers. For this reason, the Jewish philosopher Emmanuel Levinas argues that ethics precedes being; that is, the moral reality of the face-to-face encounter precedes any experience of existence.[3] A moral summoning takes place within the face-to-face encounter, even before a self takes shape. That other summons me to care and be for the other. Self-consciousness does not constitute itself; rather, "my inescapable and incontrovertible answerability to the other . . . makes me an individual 'I.' "[4] This moral summoning comes from the irreducible Other, beyond being, beyond existence—from the Infinite.

The biblical narrator, as is frequently the case, tells the listener who these strangers are, but the main characters do not know. This pattern in the biblical narrative suggests that it makes a difference how I view the stranger. If I view the stranger from my own perspective, I will not see the presence of the Infinite, the Other, God, through the stranger. If, however, I view the stranger from the perspective of the biblical narrator, I will see the presence of God through the stranger. When I encounter the other in the face-to-face encounter, I encounter the irreducible Other, the ultimate Stranger. As Levinas writes: "The religious discourse that precedes all religious discourse is not dialogue. It is the 'here I am' said to a neighbour to whom I am given over, by which I announce peace, that is, my responsibility for the other. 'Creating . . . the fruit of the lips. Peace, peace to the far and to the near, says the Lord.' "[5] When we hear and respond to this word of command and summons from the other, we come to be the-one-for-the-other: self constructed within the metaphor of hospitality to the stranger.

Within the face-to-face encounter with the other, the voice of the Other urges, compels,[6] even commands[7] me to hospitality to the stranger. The face of the other, the physical presence of the other, lays claim to my concern and care. The other invites my attention and concern. If I fail to give it, the other compels it. If I still fail to give it, the other commands my care and concern.

Abraham and Sarah do not know who they are hosting. They are simply obeying the command of God to be hospitable to the stranger. They are living out the Torah of God, written on their hearts, as they come face-to-face with the stranger. Abraham and Sarah, like so many bedouins to this day, lived and died by the tradition of hospitality to the stranger.

The face-to-face encounter with the stranger as the other is a matter of death and life. Ethicist Thomas Ogletree describes this threat as decentering of the self.[8] The encounter with the stranger as the other decenters the individual's reality. So intense is this decentering that Jean-Paul Sartre describes this encounter with the other as a shock.[9]

In a story from *Being and Nothingness,* Sartre describes a man looking through a keyhole. He is so totally absorbed in the scene he is viewing that he is unaware of what he is doing. Suddenly, from behind, he hears a footstep. Someone else is coming. He will now be caught in the act of spying. He feels no guilt about some wrongdoing but shame that he is being judged by another, who will define, interpret, assess, and evaluate his action. He will become an object of that consciousness and so lose control over the meaning of his own being.

In the encounter between Barbara Whiterabbit and me, I too felt exposed to another center of consciousness. She was defining, interpreting, assessing, and evaluating my horizon, my way of living, thinking, and believing. Such a stranger unavoidably decenters. We cannot pretend that we define our own life and values. Someone else is judging us, someone we cannot control or escape.

Sartre sees this decentering as a threat to personal integrity. When we encounter the other as a value and a meaning-making center, we may wish to eliminate it—perhaps not in an obviously brutal way, by murdering the political or religious dissident, but in a less obvious way, by projecting our self upon the other in an effort to wipe out his or her difference. Intimacy, through this technique of projection, can thus simply erase and destroy the other, rather than supporting that person. When we recognize this desire on our part to eliminate the other, we are both shamed and fearful. We are shamed, because we are reproached by the other whom we desire to negate; we are fearful because we know that the other wants to obliterate us as well. Violence—both physical and emotional—is real.

Whereas Sartre sees this decentering as a threat to personal integrity, the biblical vision presents it as a summons to take the other into account. My egocentricity—that is, my location of my self as the decisive and controlling reference point for meaning and value of the world—is called into question on behalf of the other. Furthermore, the biblical vision invites me to give up my self to the point of opening up myself to the perspective of the stranger.

That willingness is what allows us to share meaning as well as to perceive difference. In contrast to the ideology of intimacy, which ultimately wishes to nullify plurality, hospitality to the stranger recognizes Sartre's decentering shock as the opportunity for plurality, abundance of meaning, and value. Rather than simply pronouncing us intimates, I must approach the world of another's meaning with a willingness to learn, to be taught, and finally to recognize the other precisely as other, not to reduce that one to an experience, a moment in my education or maturation.

That vision, however, has certain preconditions. First, there must be justice, or equal access to that company of strangers, equal opportunity for each center of meaning and value to speak. Without justice, the search for truth is impossible. Truth must be viewed from various angles of vision; it is a vast universe to be sought.[10] Second, I cannot risk unless my very self does not hate itself or resent others or its situation. As Saul Bellow puts it in his first novel, "All of us wish to give ourselves to another; most of us end up throwing ourselves away."[11] Giving oneself to the stranger is not throwing oneself away, out of despair or anger, but giving oneself out of delight in God's gift of the stranger. Neither a desperate need nor even a command from a loving God can accomplish hospitality to the stranger. Only in faith and hope can I be given to another.

In addition, to open myself and be given to the stranger is not to demand or to pretend intimate knowledge of the other's interior self. According to Ogletree, "Such language suggests a suffocating familiarity inappropriate to the infinity which characterizes the human form of being."[12] Rather, opening up my private world to the stranger's world is no more making that world mine than it is making my world that person's; it is opening my world up to the meanings and values we can share and those we cannot, those that I cannot assimilate to myself.

In sum, the face-to-face encounter is fraught with both danger and promise. Since the face of the stranger cannot, without remainder, be reduced to analogies of my experience, cannot be held within the horizon of my experience, it remains an open horizon; it is an encounter with the eschatological.[13]

Blessings of Life among Strangers

Against this life given for the other envisioned by the biblical narrative, the ideology of intimacy accepts the Victorian image of the public place as cold and empty, a place within which men are free to develop, but a place not suitable for morally sensitive creatures, such as women and children. It leaves individuals alone in their private bubbles rushing through this cold and empty public space. When it tries to overcome the coldness and emptiness of that fearful and shameful place, it does so by denial and projection. Following the irrationalists, the ideology denies the value of impersonal, public association, life among strangers; it projects upon the public the metaphor of home or family, a warm, private imagery.

As mentioned in chapter 1, three tenets are crucial to this ideology. First, an enduring, profound human relationship of closeness and warmth is the most—or only—valuable experience that life affords. Second, we can achieve such a relationship only through personal effort and will. Third, the purpose of life is to develop most fully our individual personalities, a project that can be accomplished only through such intimate relationships.

The biblical vision stands in sharp contrast to the ideology of intimacy at this social and psychological level. Rather than projecting the private onto the public, it opens the door for the stranger. The biblical vision affirms impersonal, public interaction through the command of hospitality to the stranger.

Hospitality to the stranger implies wisdom, love, and justice—rather than intimacy, warmth, and familiarity—in our dealings with others in public. The impersonal justice and love required by the biblical command is not impersonal in the sense of being unkind, unloving, or unfeeling, but it specifically does not depend upon a personal history or ties between those interacting in the public, the exchange of one's most intimate thoughts and feelings, or the physical intimacy common among family or friends. It treats interaction without a demand for friendship as a virtue.

Such impersonal regard for the stranger—such distance, we may even say—is necessary if one is to respect the difference between the self and the stranger. Rather than seeking oneness, a pull that would surround and coerce the stranger, the public actor hospitably appreciates that irreducible difference. The public actor engages but does not engulf the stranger.

The implications of the public virtues of hospitality to the stranger for multicultural interaction can be mentioned only briefly.[14] These implications are perhaps some of the most significant for our present situation. The recognition of the need to be hospitable even in the face of irreducible differences among different groups of people and the need to develop rituals of hospitality for the public interaction among these groups of people represents a central challenge to public life in contemporary North America. For too long the ideology of intimacy, in the form of the melting-pot metaphor, has effectively excluded those people groups who refuse to be melted. Recent years have seen the emergence of different imagery, such as Jesse Jackson's "vegetable stew," for depicting the nature of multicultural public interaction. The struggle to find equally accessible alternatives that gather together for our common life the necessary public virtues of hospitality to the stranger remains a critical but unfinished agenda.

Attention to public virtues for a multicultural society draws attention to the essential importance of public structures that mediate these relationships, such as rituals and public offices. The ideology of intimacy would have us denigrate public rituals and offices. It understands bureaucracy (literally, the power of office) as a meaningless maze of cold, sterile places of shame. By contrast, hospitality to the stranger sees bureaucracy as the location where the power resides, not so much to provide personal contact, but to exercise impersonal but genuine hospitality. We commonly view bureaucrats as though they were functioning within a meaningless maze, which we often take as proof that we should view society through the ideology of intimacy. That we often experience bureaucrats in such a manner, however, is evidence simply of the perverse power of the ideology of intimacy. It has become a self-fulfilling prophecy.[15]

Indeed, if we are to understand public life in general and the church's work and worship as public, we will change our present theological emphasis from that of the intimate society. Under the influence of the ideology of intimacy, in the modern period we focus on redemption to the neglect of God's other good works, a preoccupation that parallels and abets the ideology of intimacy. The Scriptures teach that God's primal work is in creating, not redeeming.[16] People, therefore, are primally stewards of creation and only secondarily the objects of God's salvation.[17] Our redemption is critical precisely because it frees us to be a part of God's creative and sanctifying activity in the world, both in its private and public dimensions.[18] As free people, as stewards of creation, we are sanctified to an ever greater communion with God, not apart from our creaturely selves but precisely through them. This stewardship of creation is as much a public as a private activity.

To understand God's activity only as saving activity is to empty our lives and our neighbors' lives of our profound connection with God's activity of creating. We live in relationship to God in our church activities, but not at work, home, or play. We imagine that ushering at church pleases God but assume that repairing streets or trading stocks is of little or no importance to God.

I remember how this neglect of God's creating action affected an accountant for a small-town grain elevator in Iowa. At a church retreat, he was asked to describe what he was doing at 10:00 A.M. on Sunday and 9:00 A.M. on Tuesday, and also to report on what God was doing at the same times. He was readily able to explain what he was doing at both times. He could also imagine what God was doing Sunday morning. But he could not imagine what God was doing when he was trying to balance the firm's books on Tuesday morning.

I suggested to him that on Tuesday, God was urging him to be honest and was supporting his skills and knowledge of the business and accounting. God was creating a trustworthy world. God was, along with this steward, making it possible for people to trust their grain elevator dealer. God and this steward were keeping the expenses of the middle-persons down, so that bread would be less expensive. By creating a public system of trust, through holding people accountable, this accountant freed the farmer and the middleperson to risk smaller profit margins and allowed the consumers, such as welfare mothers and their children on the South Side of Chicago, to purchase bread relatively cheaply. In effect, Dennis was feeding children on the South Side of Chicago through his impersonal, public office as an accountant.

Theologically and theocentrically put, God is not always redeeming and sanctifying in every time and place. But God is always creating. When we create in accordance with God's will, we too are engaged with what God does most often. When I suggested this, Dennis's eyes opened very wide. Later he told me it was the first time he had ever heard that what he did as an accountant was an important part of God's activity. Even such an impersonal, public work as accounting can be done according to God's will, and in such work, God is powerfully pleased.

This attitude toward the work of the public life is doctrinally undergirded by the doctrine of the Trinity.[19] In the public world, the triune God creates, redeems, and sanctifies in ways not possible solely in the private world. By emphasizing that God opens us to the public world through this creative, redemptive, and sanctifying activity, we can guard against the tempting move to privatize faith, to think exclusively in the intimate language of the Jesus in our hearts.

Only in faith and hope, however, can I afford to be for the other. The threat of the other is real. The summons of the Other through the face-to-face encounter to hospitality to the stranger does not necessarily lead to being for the other. It may lead to some physical and emotional hospitality, but it does not lead to full spiritual hospitality to the stranger, life led for the other. It leads, in fact, to systems of self-justification; that is, when confronted with the command to be hospitable to the stranger, the self seeks to legitimate its status as the center of reality. It develops systems of self-justification before the Other. These systems of self-justification all share the urge to totalize the understanding of all of reality within analogies to the experience of the self. In social and psychological terms this urge shows itself in sexism, racism, and classism.

When this self-justification takes the shape of sexism, the male self face-to-face before the irreducible otherness of the female reduces her to analogies of the male self. It can be as blunt as the experience of my wife in her anatomy class in medical school. In each class period all the examples for the human anatomy were given in terms of the male anatomy with passing comments such as, "The female anatomy is rough-ly analogous." Less obvious, but still as pervasive, are the systems of evaluation for promotion in school and job that draw all their analogies from male experience and evaluative criteria or that develop psycho-logical or moral-developmental theories on the basis of male experience as the norm.[20] More subtly, by the move to romantic intimacy, the male may project himself upon the female, saying that they are really just alike, that they have become one, although it is a becoming one on his terms.

Though the dynamics of making one's self the center take significantly different shapes in racism and classism, they reflect the same bondage of the self to justify its place as the center of reality. The destructive effects of this self-justifying behavior on others, as well as on ourselves, are especially apparent when those of us who exercise economic, social, political, and moral power are caught up by the attempt to justify ourselves.

Those with this power act as if such power grants special privilege. That privilege causes us, intentionally and unintentionally, to promote racism and classism and to profit from them. From privilege, we reduce human beings to a color or a country or a class, or we construct a world that ignores the shame of a young, indigent mother, the anger of an unemployed youth of color, and the confusion and fear of an aging immigrant couple. We blind our eyes to the rich talent of the stranger; we close our ears to the wise counsel of the other. Even with the best of religious intentions, we who preach and teach in the church from positions of power intentionally and unintentionally abet racism and classism, and we benefit from them.

If we are to take seriously the systemic distortion of human communication and interaction in the world as we know it,[21] then we need to recognize the all-encompassing power of this urge to totalize at every level. No one escapes it, either as victim or victimizer. Some are more one than the other; some have more responsibility because they have more access to the resources for change, but all are caught in these systemic distortions. They all begin with and depend upon the individual's response to the face-to-face encounter with the other. Without addressing the self's turn to the self at that critical juncture, the best we can expect to accomplish is a lessening of the distortion and injustice it creates. While such amelioration is morally demanded, the biblical vision offers much more.

The God who appeared to Abraham and Sarah at the oaks of Mamre through three strangers is revealed not only as a God who commands hospitality to the stranger but as a Host who makes great and abundant promises and makes good on those promises. Ultimately, this God gives, as a gracious Host, what is demanded. At Mamre this Stranger-turned-Host promised that Sarah would have a child within a year. As unlikely as that promise was, it came to pass.

In the pregnancy and birth of Isaac, this commanding and promising Other was fulfilling a promise revealed to Abraham in an earlier encounter. The Lord took Abraham out under the night sky and promised, "Look toward heaven and count the stars, if you are able to count them." Then God said, "So shall your descendants be." Abraham "believed the LORD; and the LORD reckoned it to him as righteousness" (Gen. 15:5-6).

Abraham wondered how he would possess this promise and the land that the Lord also promised. At that point the Lord commanded, "Bring me a heifer three years old, a female goat three years old, a ram three years old, a turtledove, and a young pigeon." Abraham then "brought him all these and cut them in two, laying each half over against the other; but he did not cut the birds in two" (Gen. 15:9-10). Then the Lord caused a deep sleep to come upon him, a sleep identical to the sleep of Adam when God took out a rib and brought Eve from his body. And while Abraham was asleep, the Lord promised deliverance to the children of Abraham, who would be slaves in a land "not theirs," and the Lord made a covenant with Abraham (vv. 13-16). Then, as the Lord was making this covenant, "a smoking fire pot and a flaming torch passed between these pieces" (v. 17).

At first the behavior of Abraham and the Lord may seem odd and unrelated to what has taken place. This ritual slaughter of animals was traditionally done between two unequally powerful rulers. The stronger would direct the weaker to slaughter and cut the animals in half. Then the weaker would walk through the middle of these slaughtered animals, as if to say, "If this covenant is broken, may it be done to me, as it has been done unto these animals. May I be drawn and halved."

The story, however, between Abraham and the Lord has a strange reversal. Rather than Abraham, the lesser one, being asked to walk between the halved animals, he is put into a deep sleep. While in that deep sleep, the Lord, in the form of a burning pot, passes through the halved animals. It is the Lord who says in effect, "If this covenant is broken, may it be done to me, as it has been done unto these animals. May I be drawn and halved."

This strange reversal is typical of the God revealed in the biblical narrative, a God who not only commands hospitality to the stranger but promises and even offers to pay the price, if the covenantal relationship between God and the people of God goes wrong.[22] This God of Abraham and Sarah will do anything to sustain a faithful relationship with the chosen people of God (Hosea 11). This God would be known as generous Host and merciful Judge and go to all means within reach to be so known and experienced.[23]

For Christians, this commanding, promising, and passionate God, revealed to Abraham and Sarah through their hospitality to the three guests at the oaks of Mamre, is ultimately revealed and embodied in the fate and ministry of Jesus of Nazareth, whom we call the Christ. In his fate and ministry Jesus Christ reveals an Other who cannot without remainder be reduced to analogies of our own experience. In Jesus of Nazareth God gives God's own self, not only as the One who commands hospitality to the stranger, but also as the Host who gives what is commanded. In this ministry, Jesus embodies a hospitality to the stranger that we on our own cannot achieve. As he depends upon the generosity of others and gives of all his own, he fulfills the promises made to Abraham and Sarah and their children forever.

He gives to others even to the point of losing his own life. The logic of his life is one of self-expenditure.[24] His death, while like ours, is not like ours. In our death, death apart from life in God, there is only defeat. In Jesus, death as death, or perishability, is taken into God's own life, and death becomes victory.[25] Jesus' resurrection involves more than resuscitation to life—there is a new creation and way of being in the world.[26]

In the cross and resurrection a great exchange takes place. His death is substituted for ours; his life for ours; his resurrection for ours. God breaks through the self-justifying systems that hold humans in bondage. God is revealed through this logic of self-expenditure. God as God is revealed in God's own self as a community of self-expenditure and need: a Father who needs a Son, a Father and a Son who need a Holy Spirit to make them one God. God is revealed as a community consisting of a Father who welcomes the other of a Son, who are joined with the Holy Spirit in a community of hospitality. God's identity is not in solitary, egocentric selfhood but in a community of need and self-expenditure on behalf of the other.

Salvation is being grasped into this divine life, this God breaking through to our lives. This salvation begins by our sharing his death and being given his resurrection. When we share his death, we also share his resurrection. It is precisely this sharing of his death that we might share his resurrection that is the central concern of Christian evangelism and conversion. Participation in this great Paschal mystery is the center of Christian conversion and baptism. The language of death and life, dying and rising, seems extreme only if one forgets the crisis addressed by the Paschal mystery.[27]

As I have argued, the drive of the self in the face-to-face encounter is to reduce the other to analogies of the self and to justify this reduction of the other through violence against the other, through either overt physical, emotional, and spiritual violence or the more covert violence of projecting intimacy upon the other. The various systems of self-justification show themselves on the social and psychological levels as sexism, racism, and classism. A profound change and reversal must therefore take place in this self-justifying, egocentric self. It must die and be reborn a self-for-the-other.

Such is the intent of Christian conversion, a conversion so profound that Paul describes it as dying and rising to new life (Rom. 6:5). Through this conversion, the Christian egocentric self dies not to any stranger but to God through Christ in the power of the Holy Spirit. This death of self-justifying self results in the gaining of a new identity in Christ.

Baptism begins and baptismal discipline continues this conversion.[28] Through God's word of promise in baptism, our egocentric, self-justifying self is drowned, and the great exchange accomplished in the fate and ministry of Jesus becomes the identity of the born-again Christian, a self-for-the-other. In the word and sacraments, this baptismal discipline continues daily, as God is both proclaimed and made manifest.[29]

As individuals are diverse, so conversion can take many shapes. It can appear to happen in one particular moment; it can arise gradually but with distinct moments of change; or it can grow almost imperceptibly over a lifetime. To suggest otherwise, by requiring a specified kind of conversion, such as a once-in-a-lifetime spectacular vision, is to reject the Spirit's creativity and disrespectfully to simplify the diversity of human nature. It is thus to deny the essentially public character of the gospel and the church created and sustained by it.[30]

The presence of this self-giving, self-sacrificing God who seeks through word and sacrament to effect this great exchange and conversion of the self-justifying and egocentric self determines the identity and logic of the ministry of the church and authorizes its unique ministry.[31] The church sees itself as an evangelical conversation and life on behalf of the world, characterized by hospitality to the stranger. As this conversation and life, the church seeks to invite strangers into this divine life through a process of conversion and evangelization.

Surely one of the morally sound reasons for Christians to seek to convert and evangelize both themselves and others is the urgent need in the intimate society to liberate themselves and others from the self-justifying systems that depend upon and grow out of their egocentric, self-justifying selves. While this need does not release the church from its responsibilities as a public citizen to ameliorate and seek to prevent the great injustices of racism, sexism, and classism through means available to all persons, it remains the unique ministry and responsibility of the church to bring the eschatological liberation of humanity, person by person, from the root of these systems of injustice.[32] To believe that God has and is giving and sacrificing God's own Son for the liberation of humanity and to believe that one is the beneficiary of such liberation but then not to seek to share that liberation with others is truly immoral and an example of one's bondage to self-justifying systems.

The Church as a Company of Strangers

A redescription of the church might well begin with a rebuttal of the ideology of intimacy from the perspective of the biblical metaphor of hospitality to the stranger as we have developed it. In response to the ideology's first tenet, which focuses on lifelong intimate relationships as the only or most important value in life, the gospel's vision places our relationship with God above and before other relationships. This relationship with God, while intimate, is never domesticated, since it is mediated through the stranger and makes possible our hospitality to strangers. In response to the second tenet, which focuses on our achievement of intimacy, the gospel understands our relationship with God not as the fruits of our labor but as utter gift.

In response to the third tenet, which understands the meaning of life as a search for identity, the gospel suggests that Christian identity begins with the death of the empirical ego in baptism and "a reception of the self from [the Stranger,] the Other. That is to participate in God."[33] Christians therefore are neither consumed with realizing their identity as the end and purpose of life, nor do they desire to throw the self away because it is either evil or an illusion.

We cannot understand our place in the public world unless we confront the fact that it is the place of the stranger, fraught with danger of various and profound sorts. In the public places we will be exposed to difficult physical, emotional, and spiritual challenges. In the intimate society, we are generally tempted to respond too quickly with therapeutic realism; rather than confront the dangers of the public place and develop public virtues, we seek private counseling for the purpose of coping with this reality.

This criticism of contemporary culture is by no means an attempt to reject the virtues of therapeutic counseling, psychotherapy, and psychiatry. I simply note that much of the psychotherapeutic tradition is itself a product of the intimate society and aids and abets individualism. Furthermore, if the pastoral therapeutic community took seriously the biblical metaphor of hospitality to the stranger, much of its work would be radically changed. Likewise, this criticism welcomes the more recent developments in therapeutic counseling that focus upon family systems and theories of the self more amenable to the one being developed within the biblical metaphor of hospitality to the stranger.

Too often, however, therapeutic realism merely suggests an escape from the public place to an inner sanctuary. It ignores the moral dimension of pastoral care and replaces it with a total positive regard that generally fosters individualism.[34] When it is adopted as a model for pastoral care, and more insidiously for worship, therapeutic realism makes the church primarily—sometimes only—a refuge from the cold, empty, fearful, shameful world. Surely God is indeed "a refuge and strength, a very present help in trouble," and the church a sanctuary from injustice and a place of healing. When the church adopts the contemporary ideology of intimacy, however, it evaluates all ministry from this perspective.

Following the preconceptions of what "real" ministry consists of among many of our seminary candidates and seminarians, recent publicity at a midwestern mainline seminary portrays clergy predominantly ministering as mothers and fathers. The graphics focus on a person in a clerical collar holding the hand of another who is lying in a hospital bed. Indeed, the parentalist view of the ministry has parishioners right where it wants them: flat on their back and dependent upon the presence of the pastor. The public ministry of the clergy is being suffocated by such parentalism and its progenitor, the ideology of intimacy.

The result is a new form of clericalism, less obvious than the "Herr Pastor" tradition, but more prevalent. This new form of clericalism presumes that one person, the professional pastoral counselor, can meet the pastoral needs of a hundred or more persons. This is an insidious presumption on the part of the clergy and an equally outrageous expectation on the part of the laity. Addressing this clericalism could be an excellent place to begin addressing the crisis in leadership in the church, especially clergy burnout and the rising anticlericalism.[35]

The other available modern image of the minister—the lone voice prophesying in the political wilderness—is really no cure for this malady. This image properly sees the public character of the ministry of the clergy but falsely reduces public concerns to politics. For the clergy, as for any Christian, the choice is not between a political or a private life; rather, political concerns are among the concerns of, but distinct from, a truly public ministry. The gospel vision refuses to accept this great split between public and private in its conception of ministry. It responds not with therapeutic realism or political reductionism but with Christian realism. Christian realism recognizes that the encounter with the stranger as the other is profoundly threatening. It calls the Christian to hospitality to the stranger without warranting a naive trust in the neighbor. In the encounter with strangers, we are to be, as Martin Luther King, Jr. often said, "as wise as serpents and tenderhearted as doves" (Matt. 10:16).[36] This is Christian realism.

From the point of Christian realism formed with the biblical metaphor of hospitality to the stranger, the problem with the ideology of intimacy is not with its commitment to the value of intimacy. Intimate relationships can provide the nurturing that is necessary for individuals to meet the challenges of the public place. Indeed, the pastoral care that makes of effective evangelism not a momentary awakening but a lifelong commitment also empowers many relational groups within the congregation within which legitimate needs for support and comfort can be accommodated. Such pastoral care does not see the ordained clergy as the only or primary care givers but empowers and develops many effective care givers within the congregation so that the legitimate needs for intimacy and nurturing take place within appropriate places within the congregation.[37]

Even in a congregation where such relational groups might exist, the problem with the ideology of intimacy remains, since it becomes the yardstick for public interaction as well. When we try to make impersonal relations do the work of intimate ones or evaluate them by intimate criteria, we not only frustrate our needs for intimacy but also empty our public life of value and meaning.

In light of this evangelical rebuttal to the ideology of intimacy, we can redescribe the church. Evaluating the church in intimate terms, especially its public worship, is doomed to disappointment. If the language of family is to be used, certain qualifications should be made. First, we are brothers and sisters by virtue of our unity with Christ, our elder brother, through the power of the Spirit. Second, the familiarity we enjoy is based not on our intimacy with one another but on God's intimacy with us through the public word and sacraments. Third, liturgical use of the language of family of God, and brothers and sisters in Christ, must be tempered with the recognition that all people are God's children and at least potentially our brothers and sisters in Christ. Fourth, when it is used, the imagery of family should at least be realistic. I know of no family where strife, fear, shame, and distrust are not a part of everyday encounters.

At the least, the family imagery—especially of the warm, open, trusting, intimate type—needs to be supplemented and contrasted with the strong public image of the church as a company of strangers engaged in an evangelical conversation and life on behalf of the world. By evangelical conversation, I mean more than talking, though it should always include at least speech. Conversation here includes activities within and without the doors of the local congregation activated by the grace of the triune God in the unique mission of the church, namely, the heralding and embodying of the gospel of Jesus Christ. It is seeking to invite all strangers into the Paschal mystery, whereby their egocentric self dies and rises to newness of life in the triune God.

This conversation is on behalf of the world and has the world as its horizon. As John 3:16 pointedly says, "God so loved the world that he gave his only Son." The gospel's clarity of center and the outward orientation of its form allows for, at times, a very fuzzy definition of who is in and who is out of this conversation. There may be in this company of strangers engaged in an evangelical conversation and life on behalf of the world a significant number of people who only listen.

Paul Ricoeur described himself as a listener to the gospel as we wrestled with my doctoral dissertation in interpretation of the Gospel of Mark. It would be easy to classify him the outsider (by his own admission) and me the insider in this evangelical conversation. It would not be true to my experience, however, or to the church's history or to Scripture itself. His ability, like so many outsiders in church history, to listen to the Scriptures was so often profoundly better than mine, despite my status as proclaimer. His ability to hear the gospel's disturbing overturning of expectations served the evangelical conversation on behalf of the world.

Ricoeur represents every stranger with whom we have the opportunity for such conversation. In this sense, the church as a company of strangers engaged in an evangelical conversation is defined more by its center than by some criteria of who is in and who is out; who is a part of the family and who is not. Engagement with this center, which authorizes the church's conversation and life, is the sufficient ground for membership in the conversation.

This center of the company, which authorizes the church's conversation and life, continuously opens the church to the world. It makes the church, from the world's viewpoint, a bridge between the public and the private, indeed a public institution. As a public institution, other public institutions such as the state see it as both potential threat and tool of its policies. In response, the church is tempted either to accept the vision of the public place as the place of dirty politics with no other vision either for politics or for other public life or to retreat into the private sphere. If the church can instead understand itself as engaged in an evangelical conversation and life on behalf of the world, it can become a resource for enlivening public life inside and outside the church.

Public Worship in the Company of Strangers

The primal source for nurture and life for this evangelical conversation is the presence of God in word and sacrament, which is both personal and public. It is public in the same sense that Abraham Lincoln's Emancipation Proclamation was public. In 1863 he stood in Washington, D.C., and announced that "from this day and henceforth, all those persons now in servitude in those states now in rebellion shall be free." He did not approach slaves individually, take their hand, and first become their friends, before announcing their freedom. Their freedom did not depend upon an intimate relationship with Lincoln. So also our announcement of the liberating presence of God should not be made to depend upon an intimate relationship with the one who makes the proclamation. It should be a public announcement, with all persons in bondage to sin, death, and evil as its appropriate audience.

It is also personal. The example of Lincoln's Emancipation Proclamation helps here as well. Although the truth, meaning, and meaningfulness of Lincoln's words did not depend upon an intimate relationship with the proclaimer, it had profound personal significance for each slave. So also the announcement of the gospel and the embodiment of the presence of the self-giving, self-sacrificing, liberating God in word and sacrament does not depend upon an intimate relationship with the minister or other members of the congregation; it nonetheless can have a profound personal significance for each person in the congregation.

I use the word "personal," rather than "private," to underline that God's presence is mediated to individuals. Though intimate relationships can play an extremely important role in this mediation (for example, my mother and grandmother played an extremely important role in my own conversion), the mediation of God's presence is not essentially dependent upon the private or intimate character of these relationships.

The God present in word and sacrament would liberate us from our egocentric self and self-justifying ways by joining us through Word, water, bread, wine, and the mutual conversation and consolation of the body of Christ. Our worship organizes itself around the presence of this God and our response to such a presence. Whatever liturgical tradition or lack thereof a congregation has, if its worship is to be Christian, it begins its planning and practice with the presence of this God.

Similarly, if we are to build upon the wisdom of the liturgical renewal movements of the modern period, we must have a liturgical renewal strategy that takes seriously the church as a public space as well. This renewal should clear the way for the presence of the self-sacrificing God, who is at the heart of Christian public worship, and should encourage and support its reception in faith. Christians are received by getting wet, eating, drinking, hearing, smelling, and touching and by offering prayer, praise, and thanksgiving. Although conversion is a profoundly personal event, and the Paschal mystery also personal, the process of moving from a private religious experience to a public identity in Christ is a movement that bridges the personal and public dimensions of our lives. Whatever the personal journey to conversion (and hospitality to the stranger demands respect for a great variety of ways to conversion), the movement to public identity in Christ is made up of public acts. Restoring the public process of conversion within the metaphor of hospitality to the stranger is a critical resource for enlivening public life in and outside the church. The next chapter outlines just such a process for taking individuals from a private religious experience to a public identity in Christ.

6

Liturgical
Evangelism

While the contemporary liturgical renewal movements discussed in chapter 3 wisely focused their changes on bodily rituals, their strategies fail to consider the unique role of the church as a bridge between public and private. Moreover, in failing to recognize and analyze the modern undercurrents previously discussed, they succumb to them. For instance, the red current, borrowing from the late Middle Ages, presumes an easy relationship between Christ and culture. The individualism of late medieval piety reflected in the red current abets the privatization of faith already pervasive in the American environment.[1]

Similarly, the green current reinforces the image of church as a tiny, select community. Though it accurately reflects the fact that in the twentieth century, Christians recognize their minority status, the green current comprehends that status through the third century, when Christians were persecuted by order of the state. In such conditions, which are replicated in very few parts of the world today, the beleaguered community of Christians gathered in private homes is a clearly exclusive group who must be carefully screened for authentic beliefs. It offers services that are not open to people outside the faith, because they may be the enemy, and it emphasizes that insiders are confidants and friends.

Perhaps most obviously, the yellow current, which is still remembered by many in pastoral ministry with some nostalgia, depends upon the ideology of intimacy. The youth from whom it came and to whom it was directed were filled with longing for a time of peace and brotherly love, a time that, had it existed, surely could not be remembered by those who evoked it.

Much of the church-growth liturgy, the so-called contemporary worship, follows in the same pattern as these currents, reinforcing the private sphere, rather than integrating the public and private dimensions of Christian lives. Many growing congregations can boast large numbers in their services but have not developed a process of discipleship and catechesis. Most of their worship attenders remain individuals in an audience gathered at worship. While this audience model of worship may in some cases be a necessary evil in the evangelism process, it ought not be either the goal or the norm of worship or evangelism. Yet, it too often is treated as the church's purpose in deliberately growing congregations. The major reason, I would argue, is that the church no longer views the conversion of new members as a public process.

Playing at Home and Away

In reconstructing the church as a company of strangers engaged in an evangelical conversation and life on behalf of the world, we need a new strategy for liturgy that can link the public and private by focus on the conversion and sustenance of its members. Such a strategy does not necessarily call for a new set of liturgical forms, any more than it dictates the repetition of traditional forms. It does require that Christians be both *ritually competent,* or capable of participating in rituals, and *ritually resourceful,* or capable of adapting them to a specific culture, concepts treated in more depth in chapter 8.

In searching for a liturgical strategy for recognizing the place of the church as bridge between public and private, I found in baseball an appropriate metaphor that assists in describing and responding to the difficult dual role that the church plays. Most baseball and other sports teams recognize the need to develop an "away" strategy that differs from what they do on the home field. For example, if a team's home baseball park has a particularly short left-field fence, the manager develops batters' hitting patterns to take advantage of that circumstance. The large number of games played on the home field make the specialization well worth the effort.[2]

Away games, however, must be played with some eye for the uniqueness of different fields; there is a wide variety of distances between home plate and the left-field fence. Even beyond these measurable differences, a team's manager must account for more subtle but pervasive socio-psychological differences between playing at home and away: he must consider the hostility that players expect to encounter from hometown fans, their fatigue from travel, their living in unfamiliar surroundings, and the effect of hometown customs such as how the locals celebrate home runs. Similarly, those who are planning, executing, and evaluating public Christian worship need to develop both a strategy for the long-time church faithful when they are primarily "at home" with others like them, and also a strategy when they are "away" with visitors, seekers, and new converts.

Because church worship in America and other Western countries is voluntary, Western Christians have succumbed to the temptation to "play their games at home." The modern undercurrents have encouraged Christians to keep worship as private as possible and to avoid ritual whenever possible. Stripped of its ritual, Christian worship loses its public character, substituting performance to an audience for the ritual involvement of the entire community in the presence of the self-giving, self-sacrificing God.

This "home and away" strategy mimics worship patterns of the New Testament church and the early centuries of Christianity, which was similarly confronted with a pluralistic culture and its own marginalization. Unlike contemporary worshipers, however, early Christians were not content to adopt the "private home" model of worship. As discussed in chapter 4, the predominant forms of worship in this period were the home church meal, focused on the Lord's Supper, and the synagogue services of prayer, Scripture reading, and homilies. Even though the eucharistic meal readily lent itself to exclusive worship, attempts to privatize the Eucharist were met with severe criticism, and the very lively nature of the interchange in the synagogue service prevented the exclusion of the stranger.

The tension between these two forms of worship attests to the need for both at-home and away liturgies, which complement each other. While both services were public, the worship carried on by the itinerant preachers and the house churches responded to different communities, voices, and needs; worship leaders were thus always in conflict, even though they found ways to cooperate.

To resolve the conflicts experienced by the early church, contemporary planners might likewise develop at-home and away strategies, using two separate services to respond to these differing demands for public worship. They both could be played every Sunday, for example, but they would be played with different "teams." The at-home strategy would follow the wisdom of the house-church tradition, taking account of centuries of subsequent development of the service of Holy Communion. The away strategy would follow the wisdom of the itinerant preachers' liturgies.

As with the early eucharistic meal, the at-home service could be adapted from the service of Holy Communion so long as its basic structure is considered. This service, especially by contrast with services of the Word, consists of very complex and diverse images. This complexity is its strength in nurturing and sustaining a ritually competent community of believers. For the attentive worshiper, this rich diversity and complexity of images, indeed the wealth of biblical imagery alone in the service, is more than enough meat for a lifetime. Likewise, in the competent worshiper, the service evokes a complex set of emotions from the solemn to the festive. Like a great work of art, however, it can suffer from experimenters' attempts to "mix media," such as using green-current liturgical texts with red-current rules, or to trim its size, such as by omitting the proper preface and prayer of thanksgiving without any particular reason.

Conversely, although the service can be relatively simple compared with baroque executions of the Holy Communion, when it is compared with the simple public art forms that capture the imagination of many Americans, it is irreducibly complex. Newcomers and others who are tossed into this setting without instruction in the Bible and in ritual competence may find it too complex, too rich to be even comprehensible, much less evocative. Thus, unless this service is shaped by the principle of hospitality, it can effectively exclude not only the obvious stranger but also estranged, unprepared persons, who make up most of our congregations.

By contrast, the away strategy focuses on services of the Word and on particular occasions. These services employ a singular focus, pitched intentionally to a certain public for a very specific occasion. As a result, they may evoke more limited emotions, although even in settings such as a funeral or a wedding, predictable sets of emotions are usually ambivalent: some worshipers may be relieved by a funeral service, and others profoundly angry or hurt, a ritual response I will take up in the next chapter.

The away strategy presumes biblical illiteracy. In contemporary culture, knowledge of the Bible cannot be presumed, even among regular churchgoers. Many pastors have had my experience of preaching sermon series on relatively common biblical stories, such as the Jacob cycle in the patriarchal narrative of Genesis, only to be told by parishioners that they had never heard the story before.

Since we must assume that the congregation in an away service is unschooled in the Bible, we must also expect that they will be ignorant of at least church rituals in these services, even though they may implicitly understand and even be competent in rituals of other settings, such as the workplace or the home. They must, however, learn to recognize their need and potential to be competent in worship as well and must want to be competent.

If the at-home strategy can be compared to Bach's B minor Mass, then the away strategy might be compared to a Beatles' song. The genius of the Beatles is precisely their ability to create a large public who might not think of themselves as having much interest in music. Their songs do not accept the popular wisdom that art can, like everything else, simply be thrown away because it is just a brief expression of private irrational emotions. Much of the Beatles' music endures beyond the merely momentary enthusiasm because it plays upon basic, thus en- during, human emotions drawn from contemporary experience.

The difference between Bach's B minor Mass and the Beatles' ballads is not in their utility or relevance, at least in our contemporary culture. Bach's B minor Mass makes an argument; it tells a story that is not only the ordering of emotion but the structuring of a complete Christian horizon. It is so concentrated that it can express in a matter of a few bars the ideas and emotions of a succession of Beatles songs. The com- plexity of Bach's argument and his musical thought draw upon a history of culture well beyond his own time, while not excluding the profound values of his own culture. This classical and timeless complexity is as characteristic of the at-home strategy of the service of communion as the simplicity of a Beatles song is reflective of the itinerant preacher's away strategy.

Both strategies are needed if the church is to bridge the private and the public where the gospel can have free course. Both strategies seek and require ritual competence and resourcefulness. Both understand that the Word of God is always embodied. Both should be characterized by hospitality to the stranger, a relatively obvious concern in the away strategy, but a necessary concern even in the at-home service. Linking these strategies, in a way that ensures that they do not produce two separate congregations but are faithful both to contemporary experience and to the Christian gospel, is liturgical evangelism.

Liturgical Evangelism

In his most helpful study *Celebrating Our Faith: Evangelism through Worship,* Robert Webber defines liturgical evangelism as "a conversion experience regulated and ordered by the liturgical rites of the church."[3] Coming from a self-described southern evangelical believer, his book is more than a defense of his own American Christian heritage. It is an ecumenical and, on the whole, theologically sound proposal that draws upon the best liturgical scholarship behind the green current and its subsequent development. The study uses history and dogma most powerfully without losing its focus upon the primary question of theory and practice, demonstrating a down-to-earth concern for the contemporary practice of worship. As such, it forms precisely the kind of strategy for liturgical renewal and evangelism that my analysis calls for. Webber articulates four basic theological principles underlying his proposal for liturgical evangelism: (1) Christ is victor over the powers of evil; (2) the church is a nurturing and mothering community; (3) external rites have tremendous power in ordering internal experience; and (4) Christians must and do grow into Christ.[4]

As precedent for the form of liturgical evangelism that he proposes, Webber works with the primary source of the green-current movement, namely, Hippolytus's *Apostolic Tradition,*[5] which is thought to represent existing worship practices in Rome and in Hippolytus's childhood home in Alexandria at the end of the second century and beginning of the third. *Apostolic Tradition* is particularly useful for our time because it describes pastoral practice in a highly pluralistic culture, when the church had considerable influence but was not yet a state religion. Moreover, at the time of this work, the church had existed long enough to recognize significant problems with the transmission of tradition and the teaching of doctrine.

The differences between third-century Christian culture and our own, which Webber tries to address in his update of Hippolytus, must also be considered. Unlike our own church, Christianity in the Roman empire had known and would know again significant persecution. Nor did Christians have a complex inheritance of state and folk churches. Most important, third-century worshipers did not confront the two major modern undercurrents in their attempts to structure liturgy.

Nevertheless, Webber makes fruitful use of this parallel tradition, describing a sevenfold process of liturgical evangelism that he discerns in *Apostolic Tradition:* (1) a period of inquiry; (2) the rite of entrance, which marks the beginning of (3) the time of instruction; (4) the rite of election, which precedes (5) an intense spiritual preparation for baptism; and finally (6) the rite of baptism and (7) the process of continuing nurture in the church. This process unfolded over a long period, beginning at Pentecost and ending with the last Sunday of Easter one or two years later.

The Pentecost service would mark the end of a year of recruiting interested candidates for membership and would set certain congregational members aside for intentional ministry to these candidates in the next year. To mark their calling as spiritual mentors for the candidates, the service would focus on a renewal of these members' baptism and a celebration of the Spirit's work among diverse peoples.

As spiritual mentors, these members would function in many roles: advocating the recruit's growth in the faith, listening to personal concerns, acting as a prayer partner, reconciling issues that might arise, and witnessing the new life unfolding in the convert. In preparation for their role, these mentors would learn to be hosts to, and train recruits to host the stranger; and they would be schooled in the Scriptures and in the tradition of worship, doctrine, and life of the Christian faith. In all instances they would be mature Christians who would not be apt to discourage their inquirers with either their knowledge or their enthusiasm; their role as listeners would be critical.

Inquiry

The first stage in liturgical evangelism is inquiry by a possible candidate for membership. This stage assumes that the inquirer has already been engaged by an evangelical conversation through an acquaintance, fellow worker, friend, neighbor, or family member. Such a conversation may have been the result of the congregation's intentional ministry of evangelism or a coincidental encounter between the inquirer and a Christian that has created a clearer commitment by the inquirer to engage the evangelical conversation and life.

The period of inquiry publicly affirms the candidate's probing engagement with faith. It is also a public reminder that the church is open to, and prepared for, such probing conversation with those who are not committed members. In keeping with hospitality to the stranger, it opens the private dimensions of a Christian's faith to the stranger. This period similarly attends to the emotional ambivalence felt by anyone who approaches the church in a contemporary culture of pluralism. For instance, inquirers may be embarrassed by their lack of knowledge, convinced that they are ignorant about things that everyone does and should know. Or, inquirers may think that their interest in religious matters is a purely private matter, a matter of finding the right "fit" for their life.

The stage of inquiry requires a minimum of public commitment. It does not ask inquirers to make commitments beyond this stage of searching and understanding the doctrine of the church, but it does assist them in opening, even slightly, their private lives: it asks them to accept more formally their status as inquirer by establishing the spiritual mentor-inquirer relationship.

The stage of inquiry is thus as important for committed members as it is for inquirers, since it constitutes a very important bridge between the private and public dimensions of their life. It gives all Christian people the chance to articulate their faith and, through engagement of others in the basic questions of faith and life, to mature in one's faith. It also provides an explicit, defined role for those willing to be responsible for evangelism and others who have coincidentally encountered the inquirer; these persons can grow in faith by engaging one another in the basic questions of faith and life.

The Rite of Entrance

After a period of inquiry, sometime in the fall before Advent, the inquirer is invited to make a yet more public and explicit commitment to instruction in the Christian faith. This passage from inquiry to instruction is enacted in the rite of entrance. That rite functions as a sign of welcome, giving formal expression to the congregation's hospitality. The ritual orders the internal feelings of both the inquirer and the congregational members, enabling them to give those feelings public expression. Such public expression through a rite gives the congregation and the inquirer the opportunity to share profound values without requiring intimacy. The rite recognizes the powerful dynamics of fear and shame characteristic of contemporary persons' encounter with public life and provides a structure for release of these emotions without further shame.

Webber borrows from the contemporary Roman Catholic rite of entrance for his proposed rite, which takes place either in the narthex or at the beginning of the nave of the church. After the rite of entrance, those seeking instruction walk into the sanctuary and take a seat with the faithful. From this day onward, their pursuit of instruction and conversion is explicitly recognized as an activity within the church.

The Catechumenate

The passage into instruction marks the beginning of a time in which each Christian opens his or her life to the other. In a slow, deliberate manner, inner experiences of faith and doubt become matters for public conversation. Unlike other forms of evangelism, liturgical evangelism builds this bridge between public and private lives in periods both of increasing intensity and commitment and of increasing depth and publicness.

Liturgical evangelism takes seriously the conviction that at the heart of the Christian faith and of the life of the world is the mystery of God's gracious presence, which we believe is uniquely revealed in Jesus' fate and ministry. As chapter 8 will reveal, ritual is a crucial way in which human beings, even contemporary human beings, approach and wrestle with the basic mysteries of life: birth, marriage, death, friendship, and, most especially, the mystery of God.

The period of instruction, the catechumenate, lasts at least through Advent and Epiphany, if not completely through the next year's Epiphany season. The catechumenate was traditionally regarded as a period within which the catechumens were taught how to use the weapons of the Spirit in their everyday lives. The catechumenate was, much like Israel's instruction in the desert after the delivery from Egypt, a space of days in which the law of God was taught and Israel was instructed in how to pray. It was a time of gestation and of birth, as catechumens were being prepared for their baptism.

The instruction in this period is patterned after the catechumenate of the early church; it includes worship, the study of the Word, and works of social service, thus engaging the catechumen's entire life. Rather than emphasizing, as some narrow Protestant traditions might, only biblical or doctrinal knowledge, or concentrating, as certain evangelicals might, on the emotional experience of conversion, the catechumenate balances these two crucial parts of the period of instruction with ritual and moral formation.

Perhaps the first focus of a catechumenate's instruction is on prayer, a difficult subject to broach with modern people who have some religious experience. I remember vividly how upset our freshmen dormitory residents were when the resident minister suggested that he teach us how to pray. Naturally, we assumed that we already knew and that, in any case, such a private matter could never be taught. He did not deny the validity of our previous prayers, nor did he provide us a manual for concocting prayers (though several of us discovered the virtues of prayer books, both ancient and modern) or suggest that his were superior. Yet, in the next months, he did in fact open each of us to new depth and breadth in our prayers. We became willing and able to pray without fear and shame in more public settings. Our prayers began to attend to other people's feelings and needs, without imposing our private worlds upon theirs. Most important, we learned to pray together, to be a public before Christ.

The catechumenate is also a time to encourage existing and further commitment to social action on behalf of the poor. Several parishes I know support soup kitchens, which always need servers, cooks, and cleaners; such serving activities provide an excellent setting for public integration of these private commitments. Service also integrates the catechumen into the life of the congregation, even if the agency of service is not immediately supervised by the offices of the church.

The catechumen's study of the Word must focus seriously on basic biblical literacy and the skills of reading Scripture in a way that can be meaningful to one's life. The goals of such study must usually be modest, given the elementary knowledge of the biblical story most persons possess. Imparting the competence to tell biblical stories from memory, in keeping with contemporary language patterns, is most helpful.

The importance of rehearsing the basic Christian story and ritual in the catechumenate cannot be underlined enough. Story and ritual draw together spirit, body, and psyche in ways that other modes of learning cannot. Just as through stories and rituals we give our lives order and meaning, connecting them with others, the Christian story and ritual embodies, orders, and gives meaning to the Christian's life. Catechumens are thus encouraged to make these biblical stories their own.

The Rite of Election

The beginning of the Christian story into which each Christian weaves his or her own story is God's gracious initiative in creating, redeeming, and sanctifying. The primary purpose of the rite of election is to remind us that God initiates the call to the catechumen; God's initiative is indeed embodied in this rite.

The catechumen's willingness to continue in the process of Christian initiation is also embodied in this rite. On the first Sunday in Lent, the catechumen is presented to the congregation, examined, and set apart. The spiritual mentor, now sponsoring the catechumen before the congregation, testifies to the catechumen's progress as the catechumen is examined for growth in worship, knowledge of the faith, and conduct of personal life.

In the rite of election, the congregation also commits itself to prayer and support of the catechumens. Through this rite, the bridge between the private and public dimensions of life is strengthened, and the gap between the at-home and the away strategies is lessened. The catechumen moves to a more intense, deliberate public confession of the faith; the congregation, to a greater awareness of the basics of Christian life.

Purification and Enlightenment

With the rite of election, the catechumen enters an intense period of purification and enlightenment. Contemporary Roman Catholic practice calls it a time "to purify minds and hearts by the examination of conscience and by repentance, and also to enlighten those minds and hearts by a deeper knowledge of Christ the Savior."[6] The meetings of catechumens and their instructors in this short period of six weeks need to be frequent, perhaps twice a week.

Ritually, this process of purification and enlightenment is embodied in the so-called scrutinies, which take place on the third, fourth, and fifth Sundays of Lent. These rituals include silent and audible prayer and exorcism, with emphasis on the power of evil in our lives and the need to struggle against it in all its forms. The contrast between the modern dogma, which rejects the language of evil, and the vision of the world presupposed by the scrutinies is stark.

By this time in the catechumen's and sponsor's journey together, they can wrestle with the depth of sin and evil in their lives in a way that intensifies faith, hope, and love rather than anxiety, fear, and shame. The scrutinies allow for a public recognition of the personal and communal reality of sin and evil, and they join the community together in prayer and action against it. As such, they recall what is "weak, defective, or sinful in the hearts of the elect, so that it may be healed," and they also reveal "what is upright, strong, and holy, so that it may be strengthened."[7]

Near the end of Lent, perhaps in a weekday service, the congregation can present the Creed and the Lord's Prayer. These symbols of the church's faith, both its content and practice in prayer, are given to the catechumens as public indication of their instruction and growth in the faith, to be memorized and used often.

The Rite of Initiation

The end of this period of purification and enlightenment is the paschal mystery itself; that is, the celebration of and participation in Christ's suffering, death, and resurrection. The celebration of Christ's fate and ministry is embodied in the liturgies of Holy Week, especially the Easter vigil.

In the Easter vigil, usually a two- to three-hour service beginning at the onset of darkness on Holy Saturday, the catechumens join the congregation in Scripture readings tracing God's creating and redeeming presence in history. To God's promise of faith and salvation in baptism, they join their personal and subjective experiences of being born anew. As the entire congregation renews their baptismal vows, the newly baptized are clothed in white and presented with a lighted candle. This candle is the symbol that the catechumen is charged with the responsibility of being a child of the Light of the world. Then the catechumen, for the first time, joins the faithful in receiving the Lord's Supper, the self-giving, self-sacrificing presence of God through bread, wine, and the word of promise.

Mystagogia

After baptism, the newly baptized are not left on their own; rather, their nurture goes forward. In ritual embodiments of nurture and maturation, the six weeks of Easter are a time of continued instruction, called *mystagogia*. Mystagogia is concerned with deepening the awareness that baptized ones have of the Eucharist, the church, and the world. The newly baptized are further instructed in the Paschal mystery through which they have just passed and in their ties to the church. In contrast to the usual pattern of conversion and evangelism, this period tries deliberately to integrate the newly baptized into the down-to-earth mystery of the church in the world. Rather than lessening their interest in or concern for the world, the mystagogia deliberately seeks ways to connect God's ongoing creating with Christian identity.

During this time, the newly baptized may continue to wear their white garments during the regular Sunday service. Mystagogia might include a retreat in which the topics of the Eucharist, church, and world are conjoined. It surely includes a final service on the last Sunday of Easter, focusing on the ongoing significance of baptism in the Christian's life.

These seven stages of ritual have helped new Christians transform private feelings into public commitments, embodied in worship, thoughtfully chosen, and practiced in daily life. Over the bridge between the public and the private that has been constructed, the gospel is free to pass; the realization of difference, of fear and shame such as Barbara and I experienced, has been wrestled with at each step of the conversion. The process of conversation has worked out this hospitality to the stranger, and ritual has become the occasion and means of its accomplishment. Ritual is critical both in the home and the away strategy and in liturgical evangelism as the bridge between these two strategies. How ritual functions in this manner is the subject of the next two chapters.

7

Ritual
as Hospitality

The effects of the intimate society go beyond the deformation of public ritual. They influence also architecture, as many architects have reflected the strong desire for openness characteristic of the intimate society by using see-through interior building walls, made out of glass, a product of new technological capabilities. They have created buildings designed to recapture the past, but the community they remember is distorted now by the command for openness from the intimate society. As the demand for openness has failed in other areas of life, it has also failed as an architectural technique. Anyone who stops to watch can see people rushing through these wide-open spaces, holding tightly to the circle around them, encased as it were in their bubble of privacy. The openness threatens to expose them.[1]

Intimacy and Sociability

Social psychologists argue that such openness and visibility inhibits human interaction because people who are not intimately related are sociable only when they have some tangible barriers between them. Human beings need to have some distance from close observation by others in order to feel safe enough to converse and interact. "Increase intimate contact," says social psychologist Richard Sennett, "and you decrease sociability."[2]

Recently I was invited to tour a building housing a major banking corporation. Most of the space within the building was wide open.

Within this open space, workers sat at desks without any barriers between them. The tour guide invited us to enjoy the sense of openness.

Yet one secretary explained that she felt as if she was constantly exposed, not only to her supervisor's gaze, but to the probing eyes of her colleagues and numerous strangers who passed through her floor in any one day. She admitted that her feeling of being scrutinized kept her from talking with her coworkers and made her feel as if she was "on display." She felt mistrusted and recognized that she was clearly at the "bottom of the ladder," since executives (almost all male) worked in closed offices.

The effect of the ideology of intimacy upon Christian public worship is not unlike the effects of open space in many modern office buildings. The ideology requires that our worship should be spontaneous and wide open, without false barriers and formality. We should be vulnerable to everyone and willing always to express our true feelings of the moment.

For some people such spontaneity works. Their personalities are suited to conversation and interaction; they are not debilitated by self-consciousness in open spaces and unstructured formats. Most people, however, like the secretary, feel very self-consciousness when they are asked to expose themselves to strangers. In response, they effectively remove themselves from active participation in worship and instead passively observe the few "personalities" in the congregation, or those who have a public role to play. These public personalities on whom most of the attention is centered really function as the executives of the worship service. Although they may attempt to cover their status by using humble-sounding words, they remain the privileged few, centers of the show.

The silent observers are less likely to participate in a communal expression of deep emotion in these wide-open worship services than they would be to risk contributing in a more traditional ritual setting. Ritual builds the social barriers necessary for effective interaction. It provides the sense of cover that allows most people to feel safe enough to participate in expressions of religious value. Despite how things may seem when a visitor comes to church for the first time, ritual can in fact be most hospitable to the congregational stranger.

It follows, then, that the pressure to increase intimate contact in Christian public worship will only decrease sociability. Even though the need for intimacy may be great, precisely because so many of the parishioners may be living without such intimacy, the attempts to turn public worship into intimate space will only intensify the problem.

Provide no tangible barriers for the strangers gathered on Sunday morning, and the majority will retreat into their silent, private passivity. The stranger can pick up on this pretention to intimacy in the announcements, which may include familylike banter that only the few can appreciate. The stranger, who includes more than the obvious visitor, probably the majority of the parish, is expected either to engage in such intimate contact or to retreat in passive silence.

We need to give up the expectations and pretensions of intimacy both to foster public life and to clarify the means and the locations and times where legitimate intimate needs can be met. We need tangible barriers within which enjoyable or purposeful social interaction can take place. Ritual is, among many things, precisely these tangible barriers that make possible such social interaction.

Good hospitality through the use of ritual follows what I call the Dick Cavett principle. Cavett's ingenuity in making strangers feel a part of a temporal community was evident on one late-night show, when he introduced Sir Lawrence Olivier after he had interviewed others. As his guests sitting on stage stood to shake Olivier's hand, Cavett turned to the audience and said, "Someone on stage has their fly unzipped. We are all going to turn to the wall and zip up our fly." At that, all of the guests turned and followed his instructions, thus protecting the anonymity of the guest with the problem. By having everyone carry out the ritual, Cavett was most hospitable. He allowed someone to carry out a potentially shameful act in a highly public setting without shame. Good ritual does that.

This story about Cavett illustrates why the rite of public confession and absolution is so important, even if some present in public worship do not feel the need to confess or be absolved. It is not enough, however, simply to perform the rite—it must be done hospitably, allowing the company of strangers to participate. If the rite is rushed or run through perfunctorily, if the chances for silence and other opportunities to prepare for it are omitted, the rite is inhospitable. Cavett gave everyone concerned a clear explanation and opportunity to participate in his ritual. So should we.

A colleague studied thirteen congregations of different sizes in different economic, social, and geographic circumstances. Two questions, among the questions he asked people as they left Sunday worship, apply to our discussion of confession and absolution. He asked them, "How did you experience the rite of confession and absolution today?" The most common reply was, "Huh?" Then he asked, "When did you feel your sins forgiven?" The most common answer was, "During a hymn."

I am not surprised by either response. Hymns are a powerful resource for ritual hospitality. If deployed hospitably, they can help individuals' self-consciousness recede and open their private worlds to God's presence for them. They do this by creating crowd effect.

A crowd is born when a group of strangers, otherwise highly sensitive to the appropriate physical distance among them, lose this sensitivity and stand shoulder to shoulder without self-consciousness. Hymn singing can create this crowd effect, especially if those who lead worship are very attentive to rhythm.

Rhythm is essential to crowd and hymn singing. Familiar hymns are preferred not so much for their nostalgia value as for how easily individuals can join in the rhythm. Individuals, who otherwise would not be caught dead singing in public, can in full gusto join in if they can easily follow the rhythm. Play the most familiar hymn with a different rhythm or have church musicians who must have the rhythm their way at all cost, and the crowd effect dies away. Hymn singing then becomes the activity of the few performers.

Growing congregations often draw visitors and keep them because of the contemporary music in their services. One congregation deliberately models the music in their away service on the rhythms of the most listened to radio station in their area. They meld traditional theology with contemporary rhythms to create hymns that are easily sung by the least musically gifted. Through melding the contemporary music in the hymn form, the congregation also avoids turning worship into performers and audience. Hymns that use easy rhythms are hospitable to the stranger and open their private space to the public. They create a bridge between the private and the public, one over which the gospel can have free course.

Instead of burdening strangers with the need to expose their thoughts and emotions to other strangers, or else to choose the path of passive observation, such hymns and other rituals of hospitality offer a middle ground. They invite the stranger's expressive action; these expressions, however, are public signs that are made by everyone present. Deep human needs and emotions are expressed, not in the representation of any one person's momentary concern, but in a public act.

These public signs legitimate themselves not by assuring intimate interaction among the people of God but by resonating the "timeless truths of the gods."[3] The realness—the truthfulness—of ritual expressive actions does not depend upon whether one is personally sincere or authentic in capturing the feelings of the moment. In ritual, we step beyond the moment into ritual time and space, where ultimate values structure our experience. In Christian public worship, these expressive actions must depend on recognition of God's presence, if they are to speak the most profound human emotions and values without exposing the individual. Because God is present and because good ritual expression is grounded in the ultimate values of human experience, it can be authentic, real, and truthful not only for this moment but at all times and in all places.

How can ritual transform public worship, given the pervasive ideology of the intimate society? In this chapter I suggest some transformative strategies, for I believe that public life, and the Christian's ability to participate in it, are not dead in congregations; they are only deformed, at times invisible and not attended to. I call for recognition that the presence of God is embodied in the stranger and in Christian hospitality to the stranger. If churches are given a chance, a revisioning and reactivating of public life that holds at its center the presence of God can take place through thoughtful worship planning and practice.

Most congregations have a greater capability to overcome obstacles to gospel-centered public worship that welcomes the stranger, to solve problems, and to change the conditions they are confronted with than they give themselves credit for possessing. They need help diagnosing their problems and help distinguishing between symptoms and problems. The diagnosis in this book, combined with a Christian public imagination and sense of ritual hospitality, is a sufficient resource for reactivating public worship around God's presence through and on behalf of the stranger.

Ritual and the Logical Relations of Public Life

Although the intimate society has disassembled public life, careful attention to the logical relations that make public life possible can result in reconstruction of a flourishing public life. Any congregation that hopes to revive its worship as a public act must carefully consider (1) the creation of an audience, (2) the common code of believability, (3) the use of social expression as presentation rather than representation of feeling, and (4) a public geography.[4]

Like the public speaker, those responsible for Christian public worship are confronted with the task of creating an audience. The public speaker must ask how he or she can engender belief in the presentation, and that among strangers. Those who have faith in the intimate society ignore this necessary task and instead attempt to arouse belief through intimacy. This believed shortcut is more often a very dangerous short circuit; in the darkness created, the audience sits in silence with its attention on those few who seem to have the candles, those with the personality to speak or to preside.

Ritual can prevent short circuits by placing the congregation's attention upon the expressive action of the gathered public rather than the personality of the presider or performers. To do so, ritual actions represent emotions and values rather than presenting them. When we represent feelings and values, we draw upon present feelings as well as tradition and universal wisdom, through images that will speak to strangers as well as friends.

In ritual, we embody present as well as enduring emotions and values in a set of gestures performed by the whole congregation, just as actors who repeatedly perform the same play represent through sign the enduring message of the text. Those signs, or gestures, performed over and over, are appropriate to the characters each actor plays, and the audience before whom the play is performed.

Similarly, liturgical gestures or expressive actions should not refer simply to the feelings of the presider or other obvious participants. Rather, they must carry their own meaning and truth. Because they do not depend upon momentary emotions or values but upon public and interpersonal values, they bridge the public and private dimensions of our lives. They follow the Dick Cavett principle of hospitality.

The presider's choice of dress may illustrate whether the principles of the intimate society or the logical relations of public life are being followed. Presiders who wear a business suit in a largely middle-class congregation, in an attempt to avoid the images of clerical power, may be trying to say, "See, I am just like the rest of you. I am an individual member of this congregation with my own personality and needs." Unfortunately, they may focus the stranger's attention to the presider's dress, even to such minute details as tailoring or color, as an expression of the presider's personality. In fact, such dress may announce to true outsiders that the presider identifies himself or herself with a powerful socioeconomic class, with those who "dress for success." One must ask whether such a message is a Christian one.

By contrast, if the presider wears a chasuble or other explicitly liturgical garment, he or she is set apart. In twentieth-century secular culture, few people will remember that liturgical garments were once a sign of political power; most will interpret the chasuble as a public sign that represents the presence of God, rather than presenting the personality or feelings of the one who wears it.

Robert Schuller's choice of academic dress for his television services is instructive of the way in which ritual can create an audience. He uses dress to focus on his academic credentials as a means of creating his audience. His doctoral hood, pulpit tone, gray hair, and somewhat pedantic-looking glasses give an air of wisdom and learning. He is not appealing to persons with strong anti-intellectual sentiments. This dress has a publicly agreed upon meaning that he has judged is more effective in arousing belief among his desired audience of strangers than explicitly Christian liturgical dress or a business suit.

Whether the concern is clerical garb or other ritual details of public worship, it is critical that congregations understand signs as representations of value, rather than presentations of feeling. By examining the ritual heritage of the church and of the culture, congregations can look for gestures that will create an audience, just as actors use their body, voice, dress, and so forth to present a particular emotion suggested by the text of the play.

Such distance between the actor or presider and the emotion presented is not immoral or inauthentic, as many churchgoers might believe. An actor may have the natural ability to convey the most believable public presentation of an emotion. The fact that most augment this natural ability with the study of acting, including the study of gestures, just as a congregation should study the ways of ritual, suggests not artifice but maturity. It is not fraudulent to learn to use the resources the church has, as actors learn to use their body and voice and imagination, to represent most precisely and profoundly the truth of God's Word to God's people.

The ability to play and the role of play as a necessary element in the code of believability cannot be too much emphasized.[5] The work of psychologists such as Erik Erikson has produced a greater appreciation for the importance of play in the development of the child. Children's ability to play makes possible the interaction with strangers according to a set of conventions or code of believability, which do not depend on the representation of individual feelings or conventions of personality. A boy who happens upon a baseball lot with a bat or glove is invited to join the game, to become a part of a community, not because he has proven himself or exposed his life to those on the field, but because he has signaled that he knows how the game is played. Children can thus play for hours without having to be good friends.

Play moves us beyond ourselves and beyond a presentational conception of signs. When they play, children do not worry, "Is this what I really feel? Do I really mean it? Am I being genuine?" Instead, the conventions of the game allow distance between the private self and the public activity and give freedom to participate in the public expression.

In most societies, ritual is the way adults carry on this development from childhood. In our society, however, the search for hidden motives as a way to evaluate another's action toward us makes it difficult for us to participate in ritual. Nonetheless, ritual can and does remain the potential source of adult play. Developing this sense of play, this ability to distance the self and work within a set of public conventions, is an essential task of those persons who are responsible for public Christian worship. In short, part of our calling is to help children and adults to play in a society that has taught them to believe that their play must be solitary or that only a chosen few may play. Christian public worship can and should be such a moment in the lives of all Christians.

One of the conditions of public Christian worship is the creation of an audience, based not on intimacy but on a code of believability or conventions. The skills and abilities necessary to establishing an audience are native to human beings, but repressed by the intimate society.

The result of creating such an audience, through conventions of signs understood as the presentation of emotion, is a public geography, a public time and place. When the geography is public, the common code becomes so prominent that individuals within the company of strangers can move within the group comfortably, without the dynamics of self-consciousness and shame.

Naturally, no public worship setting will achieve these criteria perfectly, but they offer a far better model for public worship than that of the intimate society. Without the requirement of having to express intimate revelation, people can enjoy impersonal, in the sense of non-intimate, social interaction. Their participation in these rituals of worship can also enliven them for the world outside the church, a contribution to the common good.

8

Ritual
Strategies

Simply knowing that hospitably deployed ritual leads to enjoying the company of strangers is a necessary but not sufficient component in a pastoral-theological strategy for effectively integrating worship and evangelism. Once the power of ritual to lower self-consciousness and to empower people to respond communally and personally to the presence of God in public worship is understood, it is natural to ask how to implement ritual to achieve these results. What tactics for deploying ritual achieve such empowerment? Knowing what ritual does and tactics for using it are also ingredients in our strategy for integrating liturgical renewal and effective evangelism.

The modern undercurrents, however, prevent an easy retrieval of traditional ritual; we cannot simply do it the way they did it in some past century and expect an effective integration. The modern undercurrents lead us to a suspicion of ritual, so that few of us recognize the power of ritual to bind us together. They challenge both liturgical renewer and practical evangelist to increase our appreciation of ritual in public worship and to find appropriate contemporary ritual tactics.

Ritual Competence and Ritual Resourcefulness

In a traditional society each person is required to gain ritual competence. The ability to play one's role in the complex structure of the culture is taught as a part of the socialization of the young person. In such societies

117

ritual competence is an obligation. In our society, while certain rituals remain matters of obligation, many others are matters of choice. Many in the church thus no longer see the critical nature of initiation rites. They find baptism and confirmation optional matters.

Ironically, the church needs these initiation rites more now, in post-Christendom, than it did when Christianity was more widely accepted. Now, as in the early centuries of the church, the church needs a process for guiding people from a private religious experience to a public identity in Christ. The church needs to move beyond making members to making Christians, disciples of Jesus the Messiah.

Our pastoral-theological strategy for integrating worship and evangelism recognizes the greater importance of initiation rites. It learns from how Christians in the early church accomplished the passage from private conversion to public identity in Christ; it also attends to the conditions of modernity.

In the ancient world many of the modern undercurrents were not present. Rather than rejecting the significance of ritual competence, ancients tended to assume its importance. The conditions of modernity call for something more like ritual resourcefulness than ritual competence.[1] Ritual resourcefulness, to be sure, requires a certain ritual competence. Even as an actor learns a certain number of gestures that have a public currency, so each person who is to participate in the liturgy must learn some of the basic ritual gestures in order to participate in it.

Unlike many of our predecessors, the contemporary leader of worship must also gain an ability to add to this repertoire of ritual competences or capacities. If we are to go public with the gospel, then we will need to mobilize that repertoire experimentally within the diversity and pluralism of American life. The ability to improvise is critical; ritually, we must be both competent and resourceful.

It is not enough that we could explain the service of Holy Communion to Barbara Whiterabbit, although even this is seldom done. We must also understand the liturgy's living structure so as to restructure it effectively in a new setting.

Like a paleontologist who observes the evolution of the human skeletal structure over thousands and millions of years, we need to learn to recognize the bare bones, the essentials of Christian ritual.[2] This restructuring must take place without losing the heart and wisdom of the liturgy. Theological reflection that grows out of such attention is liturgical theology and an indispensable part of pastoral-theological reflection. Those who are responsible for public worship not only must know an order of service but must be acquainted with many shapes and ways of making it local.

Making it more difficult to build indigenous worship, our society lacks a symbolic center or symbolic homogeneity. One only needs to attend a high school commencement or baccalaureate (where they still exist) to see fumbling with ritual. Still the need is there, and the desire is not lost.

I think of the terrible flood that destroyed over one-third of my hometown in 1972. The city wanted ritually to restore order, but the resources to do so were very limited. I remember hearing some of the city leaders overwhelmed with the sense of chaos and the profound insecurity that it breeds. They authorized a form of marshal law to show at least some order and reestablish a sense of security. A large memorial service, complete with the First Lady, Mrs. Nixon, somehow was not satisfying.

The gathering was characterized by feeble attempts to express individual feelings. No one questioned the sincerity of the speakers or the depth of the pain that was expressed. The forms within which they were used, however, left most of us only staring at these individuals rather than experiencing a public catharsis. The community lacked ritual competence; we were unable to draw upon ritual resources for expressing grief.

Knowing what I know now about ritual structures, especially the power of the lamentation form found in many ritual traditions, including the Psalms, this situation could have been different. A lamentation ritual, sensitive to the diversity of religious commitments in the community, could have allowed for the public presentation of our grief, confusion, anger, and hope in this situation.

When confronted with social disorder, we also reach out for rituals to reestablish our sense of order and security. The assassinations of the Kennedys and Martin Luther King, Jr. sent the nation scrambling for ritual formats. Rarely do Americans publicly attend to ritual detail as they did with John Kennedy's funeral. Every minute became symbolic as television commentators attempted to conjure up some order in response to the sense of social madness.

The confusion regarding ritual only makes the struggle to go public with the gospel all the more complex. It is not simply a matter of choosing the best of an already-existing set of rituals from the local setting and baptizing them, so to speak. The church has some obligation to order and reform the confusion within the biblical horizon and, as far is possible, to live with the people in their chaos.[3]

At one time, the church could draw upon the family meal, for example, with its place in the formation of children and bonding of family members to one another, as a ritual analogy to the Lord's Supper. With the victory of McDonald's and fast food, however, the church needs to take its cues from the Lord's Supper in hopes of saving the family meal.

Despite the desultory condition of public ritual, broken secular rituals exist and can be the source of ritual resourcefulness on the part of the church. The theater can be another source for discovering the contemporary gestures that present the perennial feelings and values of contemporary culture. The struggle of many to enliven public life should be seen as the church's struggle as well, for an important byproduct can be a greater ritual repertoire for the church's public life.

Liturgy at Home and Away

Precisely because the situation in general is characterized by a distrust of ritual and a broken ritual tradition within and without the church, both ritual competence and ritual resourcefulness are so urgent. Even with the significant discontinuity between the various traditional ritual forms retrieved in the liturgical renewal currents of the last two centuries, these traditional forms need to be practiced more widely so that this basic Christian repertoire is not lost.

At the same time, the church needs to be developing a new repertoire of ritual gesture that grows out of the common usage of the contemporary culture. Such a two-pronged approach I have called playing at home and away. We need to learn to present Holy Communion, for example, as an at-home game with hospitality to the stranger. It is the mainstay and guide for Christian nurture and life. It too must be a public rather than a private event. The away strategy requires a more flexible attitude. It is not less liturgical; it deploys its ritual more sparingly, however, with a keen sense of working in the space of ritually deprived, biblically illiterate, and readily shamed persons.

The necessity of developing the ability to play away from home could mean something as drastic as holding two different public services on Sunday morning. One would be for those persons who are members of the congregation, and the other for those who live within the parish area.

In the last several years, I have often traveled on weekends and find myself a stranger in strange congregations. Almost never has anyone welcomed me to the at-home service by helping me find the order of service or explained even in the most rudimentary manner the order of service.

One exception was in Gettysburg, Pennsylvania. Perhaps because the people are used to tourists, I found public worship there clearly designed to include visitors. In addition to a service folder that was most clear and helpful in describing the order of service and my responsibilities, the ushers were helpful in locating for me not only a seat but also the order of service.

As I began to look through the liturgy, a product of liturgical renewal, an elderly woman sitting next to me asked if I was a member of the congregation. I said no. She volunteered in a most noninvasive manner to explain the order of service to me, reviewing the main parts of the service. Above all, she neither left me to silent passive observation or insisted I take on an air of intimacy. She respected my private space but not some supposed right to silence. I felt honored as a person; that is, as someone who was to participate in the public activity called worship. Her tone was one of hospitality but not intimacy. She engaged me as a stranger but did not engulf me.

Perhaps the most important regular location for this away strategy, outside the possibility of a regular service on Sunday that is structured in this manner, is the occasional services. I think especially of those services where there is likely to be a larger number of people who have either no experience with the liturgy or very little with the particular style of your congregation. These services are traditionally the services of marriage and burial.

Most people expect to be silent spectators at such services, and most worship leaders prefer it that way. These two services afford opportunities for creating public space for the gospel that one seldom has. For outreach, they are more important than even Christmas and Easter.

Conserving Ritual Tactics

The discovery of traditional and contemporary rituals for Christian worship is only one part of ritual resourcefulness. The second and equally crucial aspect is the deployment of these rituals to appropriate purposes. In the face of the intimate society's conception of ritual, it is important to discover the wide range of things ritual does. This section describes two basic ritual tactics: conserving and reforming. The conserving tactic has two modes: anchorage and articulation. The reforming tactic has two modes: passage and negotiation.

Anchorage

Most of the time we think of ritual as a conservative force in a society, which is how the modern undercurrents portray it. Rituals, especially in traditional societies, are indeed used to reassert order in the face of natural and social chaos by reestablishing acceptable patterns of public behavior. Through such rituals they try to anchor their identity.

Recently we have resumed the use of the death penalty for certain crimes. Some ten years ago, the majority of people were opposed to the death penalty. Over the past twenty years, however, the rate of violent crimes has doubled, and America's sense of insecurity regarding violations of life has more than tripled. In fearful anger, as if to restore order to society, we select a few capital offenders and make examples of them. Judging from the very small number of people who actually are executed in relation to the number convicted of capital offenses, one wonders if these deaths are, for most citizens, more ritual than the actualization of justice.[4]

Cult groups grow up around the convicted. The media make much of their death. Norman Mailer's *The Executioner's Song* conveys the sense that Gary Mark Gilmore's death functioned ritually for major portions of our society; it is ritually expedient that, as one commentator put it, "one die for the many." The reinstatement of the death penalty seems an example of our attempt to anchor our identity as an orderly, safe society.

Perhaps a clearer example of anchorage is the Mormon practice of temple marriage. In the face of significant social change and disruption during "freedom's ferment" around the time of and following the election of Andrew Jackson, many religious experimental communities were founded. Most of them were counterculture; most sought the ideal intimate community.

Some of these experimental communities, such as the Church of Jesus Christ of Latter Day Saints, sought to reestablish community in the West by practicing economic communism and polygamy. In effect, they wanted everything to be intimate. These two experiments eventually were set aside—the first for practical reasons (mostly poor people joined the movement); the second under duress, since the federal government outlawed polygamy.

In place of polygamy, monogamous temple marriage became increasingly important.[5] Temple marriage is qualitatively different from marriage in the local Mormon ward (congregation). First, there are few temples. Second, marriage in the local Mormon ward is not for "time and eternity." Third, permission to be married in the temple and be "sealed for time and eternity" is a high honor that usually follows after a number of years of wedded bliss and active membership in the Mormon church.

Temple marriage has become in practical terms the highest sacrament in the Mormon church. Since the Second World War, as the divorce rate has increased and, many believe, the nuclear family has been eroded (the belief here is more important than the reality), the importance of the family and the related special rituals of temple marriage has increased. The temple ritual places marriage as the de facto central sacrament of salvation. This ritual is, for the couple and any unmarried relations, the primary means of participating in the eternal progression that leads from earthly humanity to divinity in the highest of the celestial kingdoms.

The first response of many Americans to this ritual is often a smirk. We should note, however, that the number of Mormons has more than tripled since 1960 (from 1½ million to over 5½ million). When one's world is exceptionally mobile and the extended family a thing of the past, a marriage "sealed for time and eternity" preserves an important sense of extended community and order. It anchors both the couple and the community.

Christians can learn something from Mormons at this point. How might we appropriately use our wedding services as a time to anchor both the couple and the community? To what extent have we allowed marriage to become so private an affair that we miss the chance to enhance its public status? How much time have we spent preparing worship services that involve the entire congregation in meaningful ritual? To be sure, it is easier to put on a show that leaves the vast majority of the congregation watching rather than participating. Is it not worth our time to prepare special wedding services that emphasize the place of God's and the community's blessing on this marriage? Even though the Mormon practice of marriage tends to promote the ideology of intimacy, there is much we can learn from their practice about anchoring identity.

Rituals of anchorage form our identity. They make clear that we are meaning bearers before we are meaning makers. The first few thousand times our parents say our name to us, it is going through the motions. This going through the motions, gaining ritual competence, permits human beings to dwell in the symbolically articulated web of meanings called culture. We literally become human by learning, practicing, and rehearsing the ritual repertoire of a culture. By going through the motions of humanity as defined by that culture, we become human.

Articulation

The second mode of the conserving ritual tactics is articulation. To the best of their ability, people need to articulate their place within the human community. They need to have the power to experience and express human relationship and human response to otherness, whether that otherness is the world, other people, or the transcendent Other One called God.

Rituals of articulation attempt to render in a publicly conscious manner our felt experience of order and disorder in relationships with the world, others, and God. For this reason, my proposal for liturgical evangelism includes three public rites that order the experience of conversion to the Christian faith: entrance, election, and baptism. Each rite gives the person undergoing conversion a chance to articulate his or her felt experience in relationship to God, the world, and the church. It does so in a manner that follows the Dick Cavett principle of rituals of hospitality. Each rite increases the level of public commitment the individual makes, which culminates in baptism.

In our pastoral strategy the catechumens are free to set their own pace, but not free to keep faith only in the private sphere. The rites provide a means of going from a private religious experience to articulating a public identity in Christ without undue risk of shaming the catechumen.

The process of liturgical evangelism culminates in baptism, the fundamental ritual of articulation for the Christian. Here the Other, the Ultimate Stranger, bursts into life and consciousness, taking us by surprise. Baptism articulates the Christian's relation to death—to radical disorder. Simultaneously, it articulates the Christian's relation to life, to and with others, the world, and God.

The liturgy of baptism responds to primitive fear through carefully constructed patterns of rituals that simultaneously threaten and reassure the candidate. On the one hand, the baptismal liturgy exposes the candidate to the threat of death by drowning (submersion into water). At the same time, the baptismal liturgy exposes the candidate to contrary signals of reassurance: in the early church, the neophyte was ritually rescued from the waters, exposed to pleasurable sensations of anointing, embracing, and welcoming by a community, and then was led to a meal.

Reforming Ritual Tactics

Ritual also acts as an agent of change; it reforms social life. Luther understood the reforming potential of ritual. So did the countercultural activities of my college days. The elaborately staged ritual scenarios and symbolic costumes of the hippies, yippies, and assorted demonstrations of the late sixties and early seventies were examples of ritual as a reforming strategy, of ritual at the service of social change.

Passage

The first mode of reformative tactics is rites of passage, which pattern our change. In more traditional societies the movement from childhood to adulthood had very carefully marked ritualized patterns. In our post-industrial society some of our more traditional patterns of change are upset. When eighth-grade graduation marked the passage from child-hood to adulthood, eighth-grade confirmation effectively marked the same passage within the church. Going public with the affirmation of baptism was effectively accomplished. But eighth-grade graduation and confirmation are no longer such rites of passage.

I remember my confirmation. My parents had a dinner for the family. My maternal grandmother, the Lutheran in the family, came along with all of her brothers and sisters. It was a house full of German-Danish relatives. They all brought gifts and treated me in a way quite different than they had before: as if I were an adult.

In contrast to my grandmother's generation, my mother's brother and sister treated me as they did before. I was for them still a child—an older child, but still a child. The difference between generations was marked. My grandmother's brothers and sisters remembered this day as the day of maturation. They had all grown up on a farm a day's ride by buckboard from the nearest Lutheran church building. Their confirmation was so much more for them than mine was for me.

In an age of prolonged adolescence, the rites of passage within the church need to be reevaluated. Recent studies show we still have very important rites of passage throughout our adult life, but the church has not capitalized on this information in going public with God's initiative. Given the infamous midlife crisis, might we not look for rituals to affirm baptism in relationship to this troubled time?[6]

Negotiation

The final mode ritual takes as reforming tactic is negotiation. Negotiation is the ritual means by which we respond to life's unavoidable experiences of birth, aging, loss, and death. Elizabeth Kübler-Ross's study of the process of dying illustrates this negotiation process best.[7] She isolates five stages: denial and isolation, anger, bargaining, depression, and acceptance. Applying Kübler-Ross's stages requires attention to the peculiarities and ambiguities of particular persons as they struggle with death. What she describes, nonetheless, are some of the roots of ritual as reforming strategy. Bargaining, for example, is an elemental stage in that process. Ritualizing that process—that is, giving an external form for the expression of profound emotions and values— could deepen this inevitable event in each of our lives.

Over an eight-month period John, a colleague of mine, visited with Paul, a young man who was dying with cancer. (John and Paul were both twenty-six at the time.) Paul knew it but at first denied it and sought new cures. In the search for these new cures, he and his wife asked to visit with John.

Though John had visited the patient next to Paul several times, John thought their first visit was an accident. Only weeks later did he begin to see his place in Paul's struggle with impending death. His willingness to talk with John signaled his transition from denial and the intense isolation he had created for himself. Susan, Paul's wife, was relieved to see him reaching out to someone. Even though she did not have much use for the church, his interest in conversations with John encouraged her.

After the first two conversations, the anger struck—literally. They both actually threw things at John, not just words, though the words hurt most. The intensity of the anger would come and go, but the anger remained, waiting to sabotage their conversations. Looking back, John realized that some of the anger directed at him was ritual struggling. To say it was ritual is not to say it was not real. To think in terms of

ritual, however, helps us recognize the whole complex of issues Paul
and Susan were wrestling with. John, as a clergyman, became the focus
of anger with a lifetime that was too short. At the time, cursing God
and dying seemed an appropriate option. They reached the cursing of
God, but Paul did not die—not yet.

Recent studies of the biblical laments and reflections on ritual and
pastoral care could have aided this struggle for Paul and John.[8] Had
John more skills at drawing on these scriptural resources and more ritual
resourcefulness, the relationships might have been quite different. In
any case, they muddled through the anger into the bargaining stage.

If the suddenness of the anger was disturbing, Paul's willingness to
bargain with John, as God's surrogate, frightened John. The situation
was severely worsened in that Susan was pregnant with their first child.
They were willing to bargain with God not for Paul's life but for time.
Time to see his first child was all they wanted. They thought that if
there was a God and if they joined his church and worshiped him,
maybe he would give Paul that little time.

Paul was reared a Catholic. Susan was a Baptist whose parents believed
in letting the children decide what their religious commitment would
be when they grew up. With Susan the discussions took on depth. She
attended the regular class at church, and her contributions gave the
conversation a depth unusual in John's experience. With Paul, John
went through the motions, since Paul was so profoundly depressed he
could hardly decide day to day whether to get dressed or not. Decisions
regarding joining the congregation were absurdly out of the question.
The motions made a difference, however; physically and unconsciously,
although not at the cognitive level, the bargaining stopped.

It became clear as the days went on that Paul would die before the
baby would be born. The acceptance of this horrendous ugliness seemed
a triumph greater than the acceptance of his death itself. With acceptance
came the desire to settle up, which included Paul's interest in going to
confession. John arranged for the Catholic chaplain to hear Paul's confession. Part of acceptance of death was the acceptance of his life, with
his parents, family, and brokenness, even his struggles with the church
of his childhood. John helped Paul write his own funeral; the priest, at
Paul's insistence, invited John to participate.

The place of ritual resourcefulness in these circumstances is more
important than the modern undercurrents could imagine. Confession
and absolution was an important ritual of negotiation in Paul's case.
The rite, wherein we count on God's forgiveness and wrestle with our

sin and how it has damaged the human community, aids negotiation through tough times in our life.

The recovering alcoholic or child abuser, to give two other examples, often needs such ritual resources. Kind words are not enough; an embodied, touching word of absolution is so much more. So it might be for us all.

Various acts of reconciliation—some relating to divorce, for example—might be developed by the church in contemporary America. These might integrate confession and absolution but need to do more. Divorced persons frequently speak of the sense that the end of one important relationship, their marriage, has removed them from many others, including their local congregation. Beyond the obvious need to include these newly singled persons more effectively, perhaps rites of divorce and reaffirmation of baptism need to be involved.

The model proposed here has obvious limitations. Human experience is sufficiently thick and tangled as not to fit neatly into four modes. But the modes offered here may at least provide us with a starting point for planning and executing worship that embodies God's self-giving, self-sacrificing presence in a culture of pluralism. We need a sense of what ritual does and how to deploy it to help a catechumen proceed from a private religious experience to a public identity in Christ. These strategies give us this sense.[9]

9

A Public Imagination

The first time I remember worshiping as a complete stranger was as a child, traveling in New England. My grandparents and I stopped for Sunday worship at a congregation in a small town outside Concord, New Hampshire. We arrived a couple of minutes late and had to seat ourselves. Everyone in the congregation turned to stare at us. We were not handed a service folder; the congregation did not print one. As a result, we stumbled through the service, trying to guess what came next.

I was uncomfortable and even ashamed. I could tell that my grandmother, a lifelong member of this congregation's denomination, was most uncomfortable, especially when the pastor asked visitors to introduce themselves. She held my hand in such a way that I knew I was to be quiet. My grandfather, a nonliturgical sort, was irritated by the whole experience. It was a wonder we ever went to church again during our summer vacations together. Looking back on this experience, it is clear to me that the pastor and this congregation wanted to make us welcome. Despite their good intentions of being hospitable, however, they failed.

They failed because they did not have a public imagination. They did not understand how private and inhospitable their worship service was. Although the liturgy printed in their worship book focused upon God's self-giving, self-sacrificing, liberating presence, the way this congregation carried out this liturgy gave no visible sign that God's presence was on behalf of, and through, the stranger. They did not understand how ritual creates a public and bespeaks hospitality. Ultimately, this theological principle did not even affect how the congregation planned worship, if they planned it at all.

Whether we are preparing an at-home or an away service, nothing is more essential than planning if we are to have effective liturgical evangelism, to show hospitality to the stranger. Without planning, worship easily becomes an exercise of private habit, rather than a public service of worship. Without planning, good intentions remain only intentions.

Worship planning must begin with, and constantly focus on, God's self-giving, self-sacrificing, liberating presence on behalf of and through the stranger. The first, and perhaps most important, image that must govern such planning is the realization that our places of worship are primarily God's house, not ours. God is the host in this house, and we are simply greeters for this host in Christ's name.

We cannot be hospitable to the stranger, however, simply by welcoming people as we might to our private homes. Rather, hospitality in God's house has its own peculiar logic created by God's presence. Hospitality in Christ's name requires the deployment of various ritual tactics consistent with God's presence at worship.

First, worship planning that makes central the presence of God must necessarily involve more than just the pastor of the congregation. Worship leaders—church musicians, readers, assistants, ushers, greeters, and others responsible for the nurture of the congregation—must be actively involved, because they are engaged in a pastoral act on behalf of the congregation that gathers around word and sacrament. Worship, thus, must be deliberately integrated into the pastoral care of the congregation and parish.

Worship Planners as Rhetors

It is certainly easier to name those who should be involved in worship planning than to describe what such planners must do and who they are when they plan worship. I have already described worship planners as pastoral nurturers. The pastoral model must be balanced by a model less easily privatized, however, because of the special dangers of our contemporary period. An image for worship planners and leaders that better retains the public nature of worship is that of rhetor.

The image of rhetor is easily misunderstood, because modern men and women often employ it to disparage a speaker. Today, one normally thinks of rhetors as persons who are able to communicate and persuade others to adopt the position they hold, regardless of its merits or truth.

In fact, a good rhetor in this sense can convince another of a position even if the rhetor does not personally have an opinion on the subject or even holds the opposite opinion. In this popular use of the term, a rhetor is like an advertising agency: it already knows the conclusion it wants its audience to make and is interested only in mastering the technique of manipulating its audience. If the ad contains questions, they are only "rhetorical" questions; that is, we already know the answers.

Rather than this popular understanding of "rhetor," I propose the more traditional understanding, in keeping with the usage of such church fathers as Augustine, who was himself a rhetor. A rhetor, in the sense I propose, is a person who leads a public conversation, appealing to traditional sources and contemporary inventions on behalf of shared purposes and goals. In this sense of the word, all worship planners are rhetors. As rhetors they lead and nurture the local church in evangelical, gospel-centered public conversation and action on behalf of the world. The rhetorical church has the world as its horizon, and its unique ministry to the world is the gospel. This ministry of public conversation takes place through and on behalf of those who are strangers to each other.

Four Relationships of Public Life

As rhetors, worship planners must understand four realities of public life, which are logically related to each other, namely, (1) a public sense of the realities of social expression in their community, (2) the geography for worship, (3) the public's code of believability, and (4) their audience.[1]

Social Expression

To keep a public sense of social expression, planners must prepare worship that presents profound emotions and values that reach beyond the particular moment. They must seek public gestures that can represent these profound emotions and values, rather than focusing on the spontaneous feelings of the worshipers. In searching for rituals that allow distance from the self so that people may participate in ritual, worship rhetors must remember that such momentary feelings will recede with the self as ritual play takes over. Christian rituals are not primarily self-expressive of private thoughts but participatory, public action.

By contrast, the ideology of intimacy values social expression of emotion only when it sincerely or authentically represents the self. In fact, in its extreme forms, the ideology is not even concerned about whether an individual has accurately portrayed a particular emotion, but only whether the *attempt* to do so was powerful or stylish. One can see such an extreme in preaching that focuses the audience's attention on the preacher's struggles to express his or her deepest feelings. In such sermons, intelligent arguments on issues of concern and even effective presentations of a profound shared feeling or value are replaced by a struggle to represent the "authentic" feelings of the moment. Other worship leaders, including the musicians, similarly strive for authenticity at the expense of the force and insight of the music in the service.

Intimate self-expression, however, is an excluding path. Those in the congregation who are not given to such public expression of intimate feelings or who remain convinced they lack the skills retreat to silence. They become spectators. Indeed, they become voyeurs of the spectacle they witness.

A public understanding of social expression thus is not, as some might suggest, disrespectful of individual feelings. On the contrary, worship planners who heed these concerns are actually far more respectful of the individual than are the ideologues of intimacy. They do not presume to know the authentic emotions of the worshipers, nor do they quietly coerce or seduce individuals into publicly representing their intimate emotions.[2] Ironically, by focusing on a self-giving, self-sacrificing God who is present, they free the stranger to choose to participate with others in the most profound expressive activity without making intimacy a precondition for worship or trivializing public worship as a fleeting emotion.

Geography

Similarly, worship planners need to have a public sense of geography. First, they need to gain a public sense of the parish, the area that the congregation takes responsibility to serve and the audience within that service area. Second, worship planners need to evaluate the hospitality of the physical space in and immediately around the congregation's worship space.

To get a public sense of the parish, a responsible congregation must study existing information, and perhaps even sponsor surveys, to determine who is most likely to visit worship from that area. Census bureaus, school boards, public utilities, and other public institutions provide significant resources for understanding the parish.[3]

While few congregations can pretend to be all things to all people, each congregation can determine its strength for effective ministry and match those strengths with the needs of the people who live within the parish.[4] For instance, a parish located in a northern state and surrounded by young families or elderly people should consider whether its "bright and early" service is designed to attract outsiders.

Similarly, the church space and the choice of service times should suggest a congenial, open place for the stranger. Congregations should consider whether their buildings are maintained and furnished in a way that neither frightens nor repels visitors. Concerns about the accessibility, lighting, heating, sound system, arrangement of seating, and flexibility for movement of the place of worship should be raised. Adequate parking in some areas may be a critical ingredient to assuring a hospitable atmosphere.

Clearly marked corridors and other indications that this space and time are designed for the stranger are critical. Is it clear for the stranger exactly where the worship service is to be held? Are the locations of bathrooms, nursery, and Sunday school rooms well marked? Are the pastors' offices and other important rooms easy to find? The use of signs and directories, even in a small building, indicates that it is public space and the stranger is welcome.

Those who seriously consider geography in a public way will be flexible about the place in which worship is held. Services may be conducted from places within the parish area other than the congregation's usual worship space. Worship in malls or schools, or ecumenical services that utilize other equally public spaces such as auditoriums and theaters, can be a regular part of a congregation's worship life. For example, the Roman Catholic dioceses in my hometown recently ordained a new bishop, the first Native American to hold the post of ordinary in a North American diocese. Instead of holding the service in their cathedral, they chose to celebrate the ordination in the civic center, a large arena used for public concerts and sports events. Afterward they threw a public picnic in the park surrounding the civic center, located very near the largest population of Native Americans in the area.

For many Native Americans, their first Christian worship experience was that day in the civic center. Indeed, many of the whites in my hometown experienced their first Christian public worship with Native

Americans present in large numbers and in leadership roles. Everything about the service indicated that the worship planners had a sense of public geography.

Similarly, I know of one fast-growing suburban congregation that began by worshiping in a local mall until it could afford its own building. Now that it has outgrown its separate structure, the congregation has decided to add an extra service back in the mall where it began, partly of necessity but partly also because it wants to reach out to the entire parish.

I do not suggest that the church *must* go to other public spaces to be public. Churches are in many ways one of the few public places in suburbia where strangers can socially interact with shared purposes without the necessity of intimacy. So many suburban areas are deliberately designed as a series of private, single-family homes on private streets in closed neighborhoods. Families and individuals eat and relax privately, they commute to work alone in their cars, and they work in places that discourage interaction outside of defined work roles. Indeed, the advent of television has allowed most Americans to take much of their entertainment privately.[5]

Some studies show that a significant number of people join suburban churches precisely to interact socially in a public space. This trend might explain why many suburban churches that are even modestly hospitable grow well beyond their initial intimate communities of worshipers and yet are not considered cold and empty. Indeed, such studies suggest that when given a chance, people can and will participate in a company of strangers.

But being friendly is not being family! The difference between these two kinds of relationships is critical. Every service must open congregational space so that people may join in at their own pace; every worship ritual must tell every worshiper that the place and the ritual are open to all. It must pronounce clearly that the conditions of participation are set by the gospel itself, not by the unwritten rules of a family of insiders.

The rural church has its own public geography. After the nearest town's coffee shop or tavern, the church in rural settings is often considered shared public space. Its use for nonworship purposes by people who are not members of the congregation provides important opportunities.

For instance, I was recently invited to speak on New Age religion at a public forum sponsored by a congregation in a rural area in Iowa. That small town became interested in New Age because of a proposed public school curriculum that sought to respond to the crisis in youths' drug abuse by working on their self-esteem. Some citizens believed the curriculum espoused New Age religion in its methods and materials. Some were pleased with this emphasis; many were not. The school board wanted the issue discussed but felt it better that a local church be the site of the discussion. On a Sunday evening, the community gathered for a public lecture on New Age religion and an open discussion regarding its new curriculum. Rather than relegating religion to the private, irrational sphere of their lives, these rural people were gathered in a public place, a local church, to have a passionate but also rational conversation about values.

The congregation who hosted this event did not pretend to provide a neutral place, as if such a place existed. It did offer itself as a place where public conversation regarding values was respected and practiced. Strangers who otherwise would never darken the door of this building crossed its threshold and found a welcoming space and conversation. This rural congregation was using its sense of public geography.

The place of worship in rural congregations could also be in other settings: on farms or even in the coffee shop. Several rural pastors have started holding services on the premises of family farms at the time of their sale, which provides many occasions for worship, given the crisis in rural midwestern America. Sometimes these services take on a tone of thanksgiving and joy; other times, one of lamentation and hope. In either case, these congregations are developing a public sense of geography.

The urban congregation is perhaps most challenged by the loss of public life in the urban centers. For the same reasons, the urban congregation has the most opportunity to provide a new vision and enliven the existing public life. In most urban settings the physical structures of public life remain available. Grocery stores, retail outlets, funeral homes, neighborhood bars and other places of entertainment, and residences exist side by side with the congregation's place of worship. With these greater opportunities for a more visible public worship, however, comes the self-fulfilling prophecy of the modern undercurrents that says that public space is empty, cold, and dangerous. In the urban setting the fear of the stranger so strongly reinforces itself that the public place is quite literally emptied of the strangers who would give lie to that vision of the public.

Even as some feminists have rightly sought to take back the night in the city, so ought the church to join in the struggle to take back the public place in the city. One critical way of achieving this public service is by having public services in these unlikely places. Instead of hiding behind closed doors, the local congregation can take its worship into God's world. Because ritual allows the ambivalent feelings of a community room for expression, however, those who plan Christian public worship might do well to give expression to the fear of the urban public space. Here worship planners should follow the basic principles of effective evangelism: first, the church should listen to the parish, the people it seeks to serve in mission, and make its needs a central part of the congregation's mission; second, these concerns should affect the strategy of public worship.

Thus, if the parish neighborhood is perceived by many as a place of danger, this fear can be expressed in Christian worship but with a focus on God's commands and promises. One congregation in a neighborhood known for its public violence has held services regularly at the sites of violence. In a public geography ruled by fear, this congregation has allowed both for the expression of that fear and—most important— hope in the liberative presence of God.

Code of Believability

Third, the planning and execution of public worship must incorporate a public code of believability, or a set of rules for creating believable and trustworthy appearances. One of the most obvious and yet complex parts of a code of believability is the dress in a congregation. As I have already suggested, for instance, Robert Schuller's decision to wear an academic hood and gown on his "Hour of Power" in part reflects the contemporary expectations about the dress of those who are trustworthy or worthy of attention. By contrast, in the congregation I served in Chicago, a preacher's use of an academic gown in the service was not evaluated positively. Though it clearly fit into a system of believability, it was thought to be less valuable in a worship setting where most of the members could not remember any tradition other than alb or cassock and surplice for the pastor.

Similarly, when I wore a clerical collar on the public transportation in Chicago, I often was engaged by strangers in conversations that both deepened my faith and gave me an opportunity to share the gospel. The same manner of dress in Minneapolis generally produces the opposite effect: it results in no conversation and deferential distance.

Audience

The fourth public dimension that the worship planner as rhetor takes into account is the process for establishing an audience. The traditional problem of speakers in public life is how to arouse belief among those who do not know them. The ideology of intimacy deforms that task by first denying the necessity and virtue of such activity and then re-describing the task. Instead of asking how to arouse belief among those who do not know us, we ask, "How can I get people to know me, so they will believe me." When worship leaders follow this ideology, the chancel turns into a stage, and the pulpit a confessional. Even though many parishioners may praise such a performance, it succeeds in excluding the stranger and destroys the opportunity for public interaction. For worship to be truly public, the hard work of establishing an audience must balance its focus on the speaker's character with concern for the character of the audience and of the worship, so that the worship always points to the presence of God in service of the stranger.

In addition, planners who would establish an audience must consider how the ideology of intimacy has distorted the expectations of that audience. One pastor of a very large and fast-growing suburban congregation noted that when many new members spoke of their need for community as a reason for joining the church, they used the language of extended family. He thought that they wanted to reflect a time in rural America when everyone who attended church knew one another and all were like members of the family.

These suburbanites longing for a remembered home probably made up a good share of Garrison Keillor's audience for "Prairie Home Companion." They expect their congregation to be the Lake Wobegon of Keillor's show, the small town where all the men are handsome, the women strong, and the children above average—the town that time forgot. The romantic nostalgia patent in Keillor's show is a clue to an important public need, one that needs to be taken seriously in developing a sense of audience. Recognition of that need, however, does not mean that the church should attempt to mimic Lake Wobegon, for such an enterprise would be doomed to failure.

Yet, worship planners can learn something from Keillor about establishing an audience. While the search for Lake Wobegon may indicate the power of the intimate society, Keillor himself did not purport to represent his momentary, intimate emotions on the show. Indeed, from personal experience, I can say that when he says he is a shy person, he means it; he has a very high sense of privacy.

Rather, Keillor is a very sophisticated rhetor who planned a series of only apparently simple social expressions of values and emotions. For instance, he used the radio show format of a bygone era to create his audience. Because he understood the ritual necessity of commercials in American life, he created imaginary products and services—from kitty boutiques to Powdermilk Biscuits—that develop the nostalgic themes of simplicity and sincerity of Lake Wobegon.

The radio show format is Keillor's liturgy. Within the public persona of the radio show host, this very private, shy man allows his audience to participate in the social expression of their values and feelings. He uses songs, poems, and stories that have been sung, read, and told for generations. He leads his audience from step to step; direction is unnecessary because they know the liturgy: they have sung the tunes, heard the poems, recited the stories.

Then comes the monologue. Without much fanfare, he tells of news from Lake Wobegon, sometimes even reading a letter from a friend who grew up there. These monologues, though they follow the format of supposed intimacy and sincerity, are in fact carefully crafted fiction. It is fiction, however, that allows for the social expression of profound truths. As the years went by, Keillor's tales of Lake Wobegon became less nostalgia for nostalgia's sake, less art for art's sake, and more an argument about very important public matters. Indeed, the public expression of feelings and values embodied in his written musings produced for him a best-seller.

Worship planners may not have the level of artistry in building a public that Keillor musters to his ritual planning. They do have a liturgical format, though, with more depth and breadth, both historically and culturally, so as to be virtually universal in its adaptability. Rather than re-creating a nostalgic Minnesota village, they ritualize the in-breaking of the realm of God. Rather than offering sentimental escape from the real world, they plan for the liberative presence of the Creator of this world and the next.

How can worship planners join this sense of public expression, geography, believability, and audience to the tradition? How do worship planners plan for the presence of God on a daily basis? The process of planning truly public Christian worship takes hospitality to the stranger seriously.

10

Planning
Public Worship

Even if worship planners can identify a public sense of social expression, geography, believability, and audience, it is another thing to wed such knowledge to the Christian tradition. How do worship planners on a regular, down-to-earth basis draw upon their heritage to prepare for God to be with God's people in worship?

Critical Theological Imagination

First, and foremost, worship planners must have a critical theological imagination. Such an imagination must fight against monolithic programming; it must draw together physical images, abstract ideas, and emotional undercurrents into a creative whole. While the task sounds daunting, the Christian tradition serves up numerous examples of this holistic approach to worship. For example, the theological imagination of worshipers in the Middle Ages effectively connected the doctrine of the incarnation, an abstract idea, with the specific and concrete baby Jesus through various presentations of the Madonna and child. Around the image of mother and child, many threads of a complex culture and the faith experience of both community and individuals were woven together. As it moves between the abstract and the concrete, the theological imagination writes the many variations that are God's people together into a unified score; it binds the many into one worshiping community gathered around word and sacrament.

Good worship planners sit willingly on the razor's edge created by philosophy and art. On one extreme, if the planner allows the specific and concrete to dominate worship, the good reasons for faith, hope, and love will remain disconnected from those who so desperately need them. For example, a preacher may tell a story that is specific and concrete, often drawn from personal experience. The story grasps the listener with its down-to-earthness, but it does not connect that everyday quality to the gracious presence of God in the service or the Christian virtues of faith, hope, and love, which speak to the situation of each. Listeners must either content themselves, as most parishioners do, with the humanness of this experience, deaf to the message of Christian worship that speaks to it, or they must search to make their own connections between story and gospel.

This attempt to portray reality is also evidenced as worship planners choose "safe" service hymns because they are sentimental favorites; they know these hymns will be well received by the congregation. Since most hymns usually embody several different theological points, however, worshipers may leave the service nostalgic about the hymns of their youth but unconnected to the overarching scriptural theme of the worship service. At best, worship planning and preaching that is centered only on the common place offers the physical presence and good will of the worship leader. Worshipers may feel emotionally moved, but they remain disconnected from profound universal claims of Christian hope.

At the other extreme, it is also common to find worship planners and leaders all caught up with the abstract ideas of faith, hope, and love, abandoning those who need God's presence in their daily lives to make what they hear specific by themselves. This worship experience becomes for its celebrants a tiresome repetition of abstract truths or aesthetically pleasing pirouettes to a passive audience.

The imagination joins the concrete and the abstract and connects the body with heart and mind. In worship, the imagination seeks not ideas but "the orienting power of images. Ideas are abstract; we live concretely; and consequently, 'we secure our sense of life and our sense of death from images.' "[1]

Certain images are more radically orienting than others; these I refer to as imaginative *discrimens*, or root metaphors.[2] These root metaphors draw together the essentials of the gospel in physical images that connect abstractions with the variety of life experiences that history and culture force upon us all.

The Christian heritage has long drawn upon one root metaphor: the cross. A theologian with a pastoral imagination like Luther could grasp with this one image both the center and the many emanations of his own theology. Within this root metaphor, or imaginative *discrimen,* Luther embodied several crucial insights into his witness to the gospel.

First, he argued that the cross was his theology because it is the source of our most trustworthy knowledge about God. As such, the cross both reveals and hides the nature of God's love. Second, precisely because of this hiddenness of God's love, faith contradicts the wisdom of this world. Faith requires trust in the Word of the Lord, which points us not to God's power and glory but to God's weakness and suffering.

Third, Luther imagined Christ's work on the cross as the work of a victor. Luther saw in the cross Christ vanquishing sin, death, and the devil; he beheld in that image the ultimate form of the liberating presence of God.

Fourth, Luther understood the Christian life as life lived under the cross: a life lived out in service to our neighbor for the gospel's sake, a life that does not avoid suffering on the neighbor's behalf. In this sense, Luther saw the Christian's life as cruciform as well.

The cross as root metaphor can reveal to the Christian how the good news of God's victory speaks to the daily sufferings and victories of his or her neighbors. This root metaphor can be the seed for abundant fruit, the clue for unraveling the mystery in planning public worship. Different cultural experiences and languages may reshape this root metaphor, but all experiences and formulations come into critical contact with the metaphor.

As the metaphor of the cross is intertwined with other metaphors, resources, and theological and doctrinal formations, it leads and nurtures the Christian community in an evangelical conversation and life. Thus, for instance, the narrative of the cross, of strangers dying among strangers, holds within and to it the image of strangers, of Barbara Whiterabbit and me, meeting before it; this image is as mysterious in its place among candle and book as in its place among gamblers and thieves. Barbara herself becomes an image, a meeting of the daily and the universal; the Greek identifies her as "barbarian," that is, stranger, anyone who is not Greek. Her tense body joined in memory with Jesus' words regarding the "tradition of men" calls forth another stranger—the young pastor who is stung with the reality of the chasm between this Barbara, this stranger, who is not of his kind, and who makes him a stranger to his own tradition.

The image of stranger shut out by tradition burns harshly against the image of our Lord, giving the commission, "Make disciples of all nations, baptizing them in the name of the Father and of the Son and of the Holy Spirit" and its promise, that God will be with us "always, to the end of the age" (Matt. 28:19-20).

The cross, where stranger meets stranger, and the Lord, who sends out to all nations, tell much about how God chooses to be present in our lives: we are confronted with the realization that he is precisely present as self-giving, self-sacrificing, liberative presence. We must see, in these images, that he is present in and through the least likely persons, especially the stranger. As we prepare to integrate public worship and evangelism by focusing on a theology of the cross, the urgency of welcoming the stranger comes clear: God chooses to be present as and on behalf of the stranger. God chooses us as God's guests, and God's people as his hosts.

Sources for Worship Planning

With the imaginative discrimen such as hospitality to the stranger in-formed by the metaphor of the cross, worship planners can begin to piece together the worship service, relying on a model that takes seriously three sources of religiously relevant information for the church's evan-gelical conversation and action: tradition, faith experience, and culture (see fig. 1). These three sources are interrelated formally through a four-step process: the worship planner (1) attends, (2) asserts, (3) decides, and (4) acts.[3]

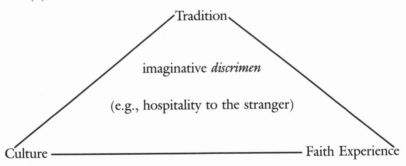

Figure 1: Three sources of religiously relevant information.

One brief example illustrates how worship planners might draw on these three sources and the planning process proposed to plan public worship that projects the image of the hospitality of God and our welcoming the stranger.

Tradition

The first and foremost relevant source for worship planning is the Christian tradition and its "norming norm," the Scriptures. Yet, church history and practice are critical parts of this source, as well. To say that church history and practice are critical does not mean worship planners must master the whole of church history, particularly as viewed from a history-dogma framework, as it is traditionally taught. In this traditional format, used in most seminaries, the student of church history first examines historical liturgical practice, primarily through texts of rites, and then applies these historical findings to the contemporary situation. In the history-dogma model, the critical focus is on re-creating an accurate history; the liturgical renewers typically understand themselves as publicly functioning primarily as historians, who apply the lessons of ancient liturgies to contemporary worship spaces.

In the model I am proposing, worship planning must rather begin with contemporary practice and seek to discover the doctrine embedded in and the pastoral acts of planning and leading worship, with historical sources as clues to discovery of that doctrine and recovery of the living tradition. Unlike the historical model, specific pastoral decisions and actions become important not just so they can be re-created, but so they can disclose the theology of public worship. The planner will therefore want to know details—how, for instance, congregations welcomed strangers through the gathering rite—but in juxtaposition to the church's own contemporary rites, so that the rites deployed will welcome the company of strangers into the company of God.

Good worship planners will thus not simply compare the details of two traditions and then find themselves forced to choose between mimicking tradition or responding to contemporary cries for novelty in worship by ignoring the details of the tradition. Rather, they will move back and forth between theory-theology and practice-liturgy, including both the wisdom of the tradition and the urgency of the contemporary period but, most important, locating the focal point in God's actions in public worship. Even within the worship leader's freedom to conceptualize ordinary church life and practice as the place of both human and divine action, the critical focus remains on God's action in the church and in the world, not on choosing between "traditional" and "contemporary."

Faith Experience

The second relevant source for the evangelical conversation is faith experience, both communal and personal, which can otherwise be named "the sense of the faithful" (*sensus fidelium*). This sense significantly overlaps with tradition, especially the most recent tradition of the local church. Therefore, imaginative worship planners must gain the skills of listening and gathering a sense of the local theology and faith experience.

As the careful listener will discover as he or she inquires into how parishioners experience worship, each parish has its own living faith experience, relevant to worship planning. Many obvious clues are available. Worship planners might begin, for instance, by tracing the history of hymn and service books used in the congregation. The planner might ask what hymns have been sung in what settings, and how have those hymns and settings changed from generation to generation. Similarly, conversation with persons who joined the parish in recent years discloses the sense of the faithful in that congregation. Even if they cannot readily articulate what they have had to learn to get along as worshipers, a worship planner who can probe and suggest possibilities might uncover a multitude of insights from them. A worship leader might, as an example, begin by asking them to think back on their first visits to the congregation. How did they feel welcome? How did they feel excluded? What hymns were familiar or unfamiliar?

This process of listening to the sense of the faithful requires a healthy critical suspicion as well. Planners must ask themselves, How has the norm of public worship become that which is comfortable and familiar, instead of the presence of God as and on behalf of the stranger? Where has the familiar become simply the family's worship rather than public worship? How can the familiar be opened up as a resource for public worship? How can we build on the strengths of the sense of the faithful and expand them for effective ministry among a wider range of persons?

Culture

The sources of tradition and faith experience cannot be understood without the third source for the evangelical conversation—culture. Despite its threat, one cannot possibly plan or lead effective worship without listening carefully to the profound power of the culture within our lives. Unfortunately, the either-or model that plagues the reception of tradition and faith experience similarly infects the use of culture as a source for evangelical worship. Worship planners too readily understand their dilemma as that of the patricide: either they must obey culture, by adopting every one of its patterns to be thoroughly modern, or they must kill it.

The only response to culture that has any chance of succeeding at being hospitable to the stranger is one of assent, a willingness to listen and understand the three levels at which culture functions. First, the physical level of a culture discloses a great deal about how a culture attaches significance to rituals, something that is often easiest to note when one lives in a different culture from one's own. Even the seemingly trivial dissimilarities among cultures at the physical level may signal profound differences in how a culture understands itself. For example, an unconscious physical ritual such as eating may, with probing, disclose a great deal to the ritualist who asks questions such as, When do people eat with their fingers? Do they eat mostly alone or with others? Do they only eat, or do they also watch television, play, or work? A worship planner might similarly want to ask, How do people in this culture physically greet one another? What is the generally accepted physical distance among strangers? Once these significantly different physical rituals for common, fundamental human actions are identified, a worship planner can begin to determine how to shape basic Christian observances so they are congruent with the culture of the community. A planner thus can determine, for instance, how parishioners will most easily gather for the Lord's Supper, or how they might greet each other with the least threat when they pass the peace.

Second, the linguistic patterns of the culture are significant, particularly the patterns that include or exclude certain groups of people for whom one is planning worship. A good worship planner might consider, for instance, what language a single man uses to describe himself and his relationship with those who are significant to him rather than simply assuming that he uses the linguistic patterns of married people, who may understand their relationship to others in very different ways. Similarly, one might consider what words create hospitable space for the ethnic or cultural strangers to whom one is extending hospitality, in their everyday experience of work and play. Do these strangers use explicitly religious language? What is it? Is it adaptable for public worship? Why or why not? Again, the worship planner may best attend to these linguistic patterns by quite literally following a stranger around, by becoming involved in the daily activities of those most different strangers whom the planner hopes to draw into the service.

A third important level of culture that the worship planner must understand is the undercurrents of a culture, those forces that unconsciously structure the previous two levels. For example, I have suggested that contemporary American culture is driven by individualism and the separation of facts and values, the public and the private. The worship planner who ignores these undercurrents may defeat the power of the discrimen by accepting and imposing these undercurrents onto the structure of the liturgy, or by ignoring their impact on the expectations of strangers who come to worship. Unlike the first two levels of information, it is almost impossible to grasp fully this third level in a culture different from your own, because the undercurrents are subtle, deep, and rarely available to the conscious mind. One can mimic the physical rituals and gain basic competence in another culture's language, but to understand the undercurrents of a culture requires prolonged and intensive participation in the culture. Worship planners who find themselves in a multicultural setting must then rely more heavily on the wisdom, justice, and love of all involved in worship.

Just as one must listen to tradition and faith experience critically, paying attention to culture must be coupled with several healthy, critical suspicions. Rather than preventing a conversation with culture, such suspicions allow the conversation partners to proceed, willing to listen, but always aware that the conversation may be systematically distorted.

With respect to culture, worship planners would do well to maintain a healthy suspicion that they and those with whom they worship are setting out to create worship only to justify the self before God and other persons. As an example, it is easy to confuse a particular worship tradition with the Word of God, claiming that the tradition frees and not the Word. Our theology, then, becomes only self-referential, evaluating itself on the basis of whether it succeeds in justifying the self. As I have suggested, when worship follows one contemporary undercurrent, the ideology of intimacy, and tries to ground its meaningfulness and truth in how a small group of performers have represented their feelings, worship becomes a justification of ourselves rather than a worship of God.

Other critical suspicions that can be incorporated into the worship-planning process have been described by the great masters of suspicion: Feuerbach, Marx, Freud, and Nietzsche, who must remain sources for viewing the planning process with a critical eye, rather than simply rejected as mere infidels. Similarly, the feminist suspicion that tradition, culture, and faith experience are systematically distorted by a sexist bias that oppresses women should play a critical role in worship planning and leading.

In the rhetorical model, however, these suspicions do not automatically legitimate an overthrow of the tradition because of a systematic doubt about sexism, racism, classism, or the other ways we justify ourselves before God and others through our worship. Rather, the suspicions should be trained on the tradition, as well as on faith experience and culture, in a systematic four-step process, which includes attending, asserting, deciding, and acting.

Four-Step Planning Process

To comprehend how the process of planning worship may be understood in its parts, imagine with me a group of Christians who are responsible for the planning and practice of worship in a parish. Even if the parish is relatively small, perhaps 250 baptized members, several persons in the parish will have considerable experience in the arts of worship. The primary task of these experienced leaders, who will meet regularly, is to plan, practice, and reflect on worship so that God's liberative presence is disclosed in worship and the people of God are drawn into and receive this presence with prayer, praise, and thanksgiving. In the process of joining the sources of tradition, faith experience, and culture, these planners will pass through four phases of preparation: attending, asserting, deciding, and acting.

Attending

To attend means to seek out available information on a particular pastoral concern in faith experience, Christian tradition, and cultural sources, as I have previously described. As a listener or attender, the worship planner may need to slow down long enough to listen to his or her own faith experience and that of those who are closest and dearest. My experience with Barbara underlined to me the profound significance of my mother's and grandmother's practice of teaching me the liturgy. It reminded me that I sat between them and learned to read first from the hymnbook long before I was taught in a schoolroom. Indeed, by reflecting on the experience with Barbara, I discovered how the rhythm, rhyme, and reason of the liturgy shaped my life.

Above all, this initial posture of listening means suspending premature judgment. The most common premature judgment that worship planners make is that they are in an either-or relationship with the source to which they are listening—they must either effect a complete separation from these sources by skepticism about the message they hear or adopt completely and uncritically everything that is said. Similarly, however, if we attend with healthy suspicion to what others say, we must also attend critically to our own assumptions and experiences.

The most important place for planners to begin is by attending to the Scriptures appointed for the day and to integration of textual themes with the time and space of the liturgical year. Imaginative planners cannot be irrevocably tied to a lectionary, however; they may well discover, particularly for special occasions and local festivals, that other texts can and should be appointed. In attending to these texts, planners must study three facets of the text: (1) the text within the entire biblical book within which it is found and a description of the underlying themes, (2) particular instances and stories of the text, and (3) practical instances of the emotional and spiritual tensions inherent in the underlying theme.

Imagine our worship planning group is working with the texts from the sixth Sunday after Epiphany, Series A: Ps. 119:1-16; Deut. 30:15-20; 1 Cor. 2:6-13; Matt. 5:20-37. They might recognize, first, that the underlying theme of those texts is recognition of the will of God in the expressions of the law. The particular instances taken from the text might include a verse from the psalm: "With my whole heart I seek you; do not let me stray from your commandments" (v. 10).

Within this image, the tensions inherent in the underlying theme become clearer: life becomes a search for God, a search focused on God's commandments. Yet, it is also filled with anxiety, as the psalmist recognizes that it is easy to wander from the commandments of God. These facets of the text permit the worship group to play with the image of life as a search for God, to ask what difference it makes to ordinary people in their everyday lives if they imagine their lives as a search for God. Within that imaginative play, the cultural images that compete with this textual image burst forth: life as a climb up the corporate ladder in search of success, or life as a search for self-fulfillment or self-realization.

At this stage, worship planning is best described precisely as cultural play, as planners let go of adult inhibitions and toss out ideas and images to others who are willing to hear and not yet criticize. While the role of culture is often denigrated in traditional worship planning, it is in fact impossible for worship planners *not* to be affected by the surround-ing culture. It thus is unwise to attempt to plan worship without listening carefully to the profound power of culture in our lives; we need to ensure that cultural effects enhance rather than detract from the focus of the service.

In our imaginary worship planning group, the use of cultural images for seeking evoke the concrete life experiences of members of the parish who seek out God and others who fail to seek him. Teenagers on the planning committee might talk about what it is like to walk into an electronics or clothing store filled with things they want but cannot afford. They might ask, with the group, what the choice of obeying God's commandment not to steal has to do with seeking God, with the meaning of their life.

This inventive play with an image from the text may at first seem to produce stories or metaphors too diverse, scattered, trivial, or even ambiguous to be expressed in good ritual. Yet, they point to the reality that seeking God through the commands of God is just such a scattered and ambiguous, even ambivalent, experience. Good ritual embodies ambivalent emotions and anxieties in images and then structures them in such a way that God's response can be heard clearly.

Concrete images—the hearer walking in the store, the psalmist wan-dering from the commandments—can thus be joined to the emotional and spiritual ambivalence one might have toward the law, with its security and its threats. Our planners may join the psalmist in asking that our whole heart seek God by walking in the way of the com-mandments. They might, at the same time, with the psalmist, fear exposure and shame for breach of the law (v. 6) as well as the anger that might follow from the vulnerability to that shame.

Similarly, the life of the congregation (the primary source for faith experience), together with the forces brought to bear on the parish (the primary source for cultural experience), must be drawn into the un-derlying themes and particular instances of how law functions in the lives of the people. Here, imagination must move freely over the ma-terial, to allow multiple connections around the theme of law and life as seeking God.

Asserting

After this initial stage of playful attending, the worship planners begin asserting. "Asserting" here means to engage the information from these three sources, allowing each to clarify and challenge the other to expand and deepen religious insight. The process of asserting acknowledges the value of each person's own needs and convictions in a way that respects those of others.

The process of asserting in the worship planning setting, however, is not the same as the sort of intellectual conversations one might engage in at the seminary or the university. The scholar can attend and assert with a distance not available to worship planners and leaders. Unlike scholars, who can stop before they acknowledge the value of others' needs and convictions, worship planners and leaders must assert.

Asserting is inherently a communal activity. While much of the work of those responsible for public worship requires individual study and effort (only the musician can practice the organ hymns, only the preacher prepare the sermon), the process of disciplined attending and asserting is a public, rhetorical activity. Asserting includes articulating a topic; expressing it at the spiritual, conceptual, and imaging levels; and making certain claims regarding that topic. Both attending and asserting require reflective insight that attends and integrates with an eye to the task at hand: the planning and practice of worship.

What might the process of attending involve in planning worship for Epiphany 6? Our imaginative rhetors have tossed around a number of ideas and images, playing with them and discovering a number of possible connections and associations. Now they begin to critique the main image they have chosen and the underlying theme that it captures.

Our worship planners might imagine the law of God by using contrasting images: the police officer walking the beat, for instance, versus Jesus wandering among his people. They will easily recognize that the image of the law of God as a police officer on the beat is a very public one, an image that a potential worship audience would easily understand. Yet, our planners will also imagine the very different reactions that the image of a policeman will produce in a diverse audience. Some worshipers will respond positively to this close association of the law of God with a police officer, but others will be deeply disturbed.

Those disturbed by the analogy may be comforted if the image of Jesus wandering among his people as the law of God is instead set in sharp contrast to the image of the police officer walking a beat. Similarly, those who view the police officer image positively will be angered by a deliberate attempt to contrast that image with Jesus.

Deciding

After the stage of asserting has given planners room to critique the different options, the third moment in the worship planning arises: the moment of deciding. Deciding follows from genuine insight and leads to action. At the stage of deciding, the skills of those who enjoy imaginative exploration through feelings and ideas and those who want immediate, practical action are focused together into a disciplined response. Most of the initial ideas offered by the imaginative explorer will not work. Still others might be left for another day, because successful worship allows the incorporation of only one basic image or idea, on which planning proceeds.

Decisions on worship need always to be made in the face of ambiguity. The image of God's law as a police officer on a beat will be met with great ambivalence in our society; indeed, a predominantly minority congregation in an urban setting might well respond quite differently than white parishioners in a rural parish. Similarly, the image of God's law as Jesus wandering among his people is not without ambiguity: to some in a culture that prizes individuality and aggressive, decisive action, for instance, it may suggest a weak God, who cannot lead his people. Others, however, will be drawn to the image of a God whose most important task is to come among, and be with, his people in their suffering.

The realities of ambiguity and ambivalence are not excuses for avoiding a creative move or for shying away from a decision that can be warranted by good reasons, such as a decision to portray God as a police officer. These good reasons, based upon insight and reflection, should be publicly available for fellow worship planners and leaders in other congregations and members of the congregation. Many of these decisions will be practical calls that depend upon experience in a particular congregation and parish.

Most of these good reasons, however, are the material of theology. Our reasons for making certain choices depend upon statements, beliefs, and arguments we make about what God is doing in the world and how God sees things. In our example, for instance, it is a theological question to ask, How is God's presence among us like a police officer on patrol? Does not God compel our love of our fellow creature? Is this not a part of God's presence as law? Even if the police officer on patrol is not a perfect analogy for God's presence among us as law, how is it a social expression of the truth, meaning, and meaningfulness of God's law in our life?

Preparing worship that connects with public life necessitates such theologically difficult questions. In the intimate society we are tempted to make God's law a private matter, a matter of individual conscience. We avoid images in our worship of God at work in public ways. If worship planning and leading is to keep central the public presence of the self-giving, self-sacrificing, liberating God, however, hard theological decisions must be made. God's presence in the world needs to be embodied through ritual, which demands specific, concrete images. Flawed and ambiguous as these images will be, they must be chosen and then be acted upon.

Acting

Acting is the critical difference between scholar and worship planner and leader. The scholar can postpone action more often than can those responsible for worship. But the responsibility to reflect theologically does not end where action begins, although such reflection has been highly neglected in European and American theology because of the modern dogma.

Luckily, Christian models from other cultures exist. Our pastoral-theological strategy owes much to the work of the Uruguayan liberation theologian Juan Luis Segundo and the French philosopher Paul Ricoeur.[4] Ricoeur has shown how critical reflection arises from attention, always in relation to the symbols, metaphors, and stories of lived experience. Thought that does not arise from, and take seriously, the need to act—not in a purely abstract sense but in particular cases—is inadequate.

Theological reflection in planning and leading worship is embedded in and surrounds pastoral actions. The execution of any decision is thus as much a theological matter as the process of attending, asserting, and deciding that precedes it; theology is embodied in some set of actions, and all actions can be theologically understood.

Finally, it is important that worship planners and leaders regularly reflect upon their past services. Certain successful patterns can be repeated, and unsuccessful ones changed. Without such reflection after the fact, worship planners and leaders cannot learn and grow. With such reflection, they can move beyond doing what "seems to work" to what might effectively extend the reign of God and the unique ministry of the gospel on behalf of the world. In evaluating their past practice, worship planners must attend to the ways in which the sources of tradition, faith experience, and culture interacted in recent services. Above all they must ask how effectively their planning and practice of public worship conformed to the liberative presence of God and whether it was truly hospitable to strangers.

Postscript:
On the Road to Emmaus

During the last week of my pastorate in a church in the city of Chicago, I was visiting a McDonald's, looking for a soft drink and fries and a chance to recover from the funeral I had just completed and to escape from the hot muggy air of a late July day in Chicago. As I started to eat my fries, a very large black man started toward the table. Being a racist, I immediately checked the security of my billfold and started to decide how much I would be willing to share with him. Without asking, he seated himself in the booth in which I was sitting, immediately across from me. Now I was nervous.

"How are you doing, Father?" he opened. I was wearing my clerical collar. "You look like you've had a bad day. Would you like to talk about it?"

I admitted to having a tough day. The funeral had not gone well. To start with, we had driven to the wrong cemetery. Things at the cemetery had not gone better. I was tired and somewhat discouraged about how I had been as a pastor to the family and friends of the deceased.

Then he reached across the table with his hand. Placing his index finger right in my chest, he asked, "Do you believe that stuff about Jesus rising from the dead? And do you believe it is true about you?"

I was, to put it mildly, taken aback by this question. Even though one can expect almost anything on the streets of Chicago, I had never had this happen before. In fact, although I had attended Sunday school since I was three years old, been confirmed in a conservative Christian denomination, passed denominational exams in two different church bodies, and taught at a denominational seminary, no one had ever asked me that question.

I answered, "I guess I believe it. At least on my good days I believe it. On other days, I don't even pay attention to Jesus, much less the resurrection. On other days, I can't bring myself to accept it, even when I want to."

He looked satisfied and said, "I thought so." And then he left.

A number of years later, when I was on sabbatical and reading the Gospel according to St. Luke and the Acts of the Apostles for my devotional reading, I came upon a passage in Luke 24. Two disciples, in all likelihood, a husband and wife, are walking to Emmaus, a suburb of Jerusalem. They are joined by a stranger. Once again, as in the Abraham and Sarah encounter at the oaks of Mamre, the biblical narrator tells the audience what the couple does not know, that the stranger is the Lord.

As they walk along, they are discussing the big events of the weekend in the capital city. The stranger asks what things they are talking about. They responded:

> The things about Jesus of Nazareth, who was a prophet mighty in deed and word before God and all the people, and how our chief priests and leaders handed him over to be condemned to death and crucified him. But we had hoped that he was the one to redeem Israel. Yes, and besides all this, it is now the third day since these things took place. Moreover, some women of our group astounded us. They were at the tomb early this morning, and when they did not find his body there, they came back and told us that they had indeed even seen a vision of angels who said that he was alive. Some of those who were with us went to the tomb and found it just as the women had said; but they did not see him. (vv. 19-24)

And the stranger said to them, "Oh, how foolish you are, and how slow of heart to believe all that the prophets have declared! Was it not necessary that the Messiah should suffer these things and then enter into his glory?" Then he rehearsed Moses and the prophets and interpreted to them "the things about himself in all the scriptures" (vv. 25-27).

Now they arrived at their village. When the stranger seemed to be going on, the woman turned to her husband and suggested they invite him to stay for the night, since it was evening. Her husband turned to the stranger and invited him to stay. The stranger accepted.

Later as they were preparing to eat, they invited the stranger to say the table blessing. As he lifted the bread in blessing and gave to them, "their eyes were opened, and they recognized him; and he vanished from their sight" (v. 31).

Not until these several years had passed did I recognize who the stranger was sitting with me in the booth at McDonald's. I take this to be somewhat of a parable for the church's present circumstance. I am convinced that the church is on a journey, on the road to Emmaus. On this journey, we are accompanied by a company of strangers.

In particular, the mainline churches, especially those with a liturgical tradition, are at a crucial juncture in this journey. We have enjoyed the company of our Lord but have lost the habit of inviting strangers to dinner or taking up conversations with strangers on the road. We have become so maintenance oriented that we fail to see the mission that is within our doors or at least within our neighborhoods.

My collar reminds me that I belong to a tradition that is not ashamed to reveal its identity in public or to carry on public ministry; it also reminds me of the liturgical heritage of public worship that seeks to be hospitable to the stranger. In continuity with this heritage, questions arise. Are the members of these churches willing to share their table with strangers? Are they ready to risk being ignorant in the presence of strangers and even to be instructed by them and have them open to us the Scriptures? When the opportunity arises, will they be willing to share the story of Jesus with them and invite them to explore the truth, meaning, and meaningfulness of the story? Then will they be patient enough to journey with them from a private apprehension of this faith to a public identity in Christ? Will they, knowing fully that they might well end up being their guests, and surely Christ's guest, welcome the stranger?

Notes

Preface

1. In this book, I use a development of Aristotle's definitions of theory and practice. For a helpful treatment of the classical distinction, see Nicholas Lobkowicz, *Theory and Practice: History of a Concept from Aristotle to Marx* (Notre Dame, Ind.: University of Notre Dame Press, 1967), chaps. 1–3; cf. Charles M. Wood, *Vision and Discernment: An Orientation in Theological Study* (Atlanta, Ga.: Scholars Press, 1985), 63ff.

Introduction: Public Worship and the Stranger

1. Kennon L. Callahan, *Twelve Keys to an Effective Church: Strategic Planning for Mission* (San Francisco: Harper and Row, 1983), 23.

2. *Constitution on the Sacred Liturgy* (Collegeville, Minn.: Liturgical Press, 1963), 12–13.

3. Worship as a form of "presentation evangelism" is a term of art within church-growth circles and is a development of the camp meeting. See, for example, David Luecke, *Evangelical Style and Lutheran Substance: Facing America's Mission Challenge* (St. Louis: Concordia, 1988).

4. Lyle E. Schaller, *Assimilating New Members,* Creative Leadership series (Nashville: Abingdon Press, 1978), 16.

5. For a clear and succinct development of this point, see Paul Holmer, "About Liturgy and Its Logic," *Worship* 50, no. 1 (January 1976): 18–28.

6. Schaller, *Assimilating,* 18.

7. Carl George explicitly rejects the notion that in order to grow, congregations need to dispense with liturgical worship. He further doubts that a congregation that turns all worship into "presentation evangelism," without also developing a process of discipling, will enjoy long-term numerical growth.

George discussed this topic with at the Institute for Church Growth in Pasadena (1 November 1990) and at a metachurch presentation in Minneapolis (7 December 1990).

8. Recent ecumenical debates regarding apostolicity too often jump to the question of apostolic succession. However the question of apostolic succession is resolved, the original point of apostolic character is the sense of being sent, like the apostles, to be evangelical witnesses. How ironic that many churches now advocating apostolic succession are quite limited in their willingness to risk apostolic witness in the American environment.

9. For example, see Schaller, *Assimilating*.

10. Carl George, in his metachurch presentation, suggests certain patterns of growth and leadership development that apply to congregations of various sizes and in different situations. Although the data for my proposal are less substantial for particular unrepresented groups of European-American-dominated congregations, the basic sociological and anthropological principles suggest that this proposal would apply in such settings as well. Cf. Carl F. George, *Prepare Your Church for the Future* (Old Tappan, N.J.: Revell, 1990).

11. Richard Sennett, *The Fall of Public Man: On the Social Psychology of Capitalism* (New York: Random House, 1978), 3.

12. The *locus classicus* in contemporary social psychological theory for the discussion of the experience of the outside stranger is Alfred Schutz, "The Stranger: An Essay in Social Psychology," in *Collected Papers: Studies in Social Theory,* edited with an introduction by Arvid Brodersen (The Hague: Martinus Nijhoff, 1964), 92–112.

13. This analysis depends heavily upon Wayne C. Booth, *Modern Dogma and the Rhetoric of Assent* (Chicago: University of Chicago Press, 1974); and Richard Bernstein, *Beyond Objectivism and Relativism: Science, Hermeneutics, and Praxis* (Philadelphia: University of Pennsylvania Press, 1983).

14. Carl S. Dudley, *Making the Small Church Effective* (Nashville: Abingdon Press, 1978), describes how the small church understands itself in terms of intimacy. When this single-cell model works, it surely is a valid form of gathering, and nothing in this book should be understood as denying such validity. My point is simply that such congregations will not reach out to significant numbers of persons who will not want to be a part of the family; neither will such congregations reach across racial and class barriers in any magnitude.

15. C. Peter Wagner discusses this single-cell church phenomenon whenever he presents "Breaking the Two-Hundred Barrier" seminars. He identifies this phenomenon as the most significant factor keeping churches below this number.

16. Schaller, *Assimilating*.

17. Parker Palmer, *The Company of Strangers* (New York: Crossroad, 1981), 122–23.

18. Carl George's metachurch theory notes the importance of "celebration," or the public worship side of the metachurch, but does not develop a sustained

strategy for it. I see this book as a complement to his excellent work on small-group ministry and leadership development. See George, *Prepare Your Church,* 61ff.

19. Robert Webber, *Celebrating Our Faith: Evangelism through Worship* (San Francisco: Harper and Row, 1986), 1.

20. Roland Delattre, "Ritual Competence and Ritual Resourcefulness," *Soundings* 61, no. 3 (Fall 1978): 281–301.

Chapter 1: Public Worship in an Intimate Society

1. Parker Palmer, *The Company of Strangers* (New York: Crossroad, 1981), 108.

2. Richard Sennett, *The Fall of Public Man: On the Social Psychology of Capitalism* (New York: Random House, 1978), 257ff.

3. Ibid., 183.

4. See Gershen Kaufman, *Shame: The Power of Caring,* 2nd ed. (Cambridge, Mass.: Schenkman, 1985).

5. Quoted in Sennett, *Fall,* 201.

6. Steven Simpler, "Causal Format Aside, Lutheran Congregation Sticks Close to Its Own," *Arizona Republic,* 4 October 1986.

7. Palmer, *Company of Strangers,* 17–35.

8. Schuller's response, however, is only to the psychological; it does not carry its diagnosis deep enough. It neither draws upon the rich resources of the Christian tradition necessary to risk an in-depth analysis of the crisis in self-esteem nor understands nor trusts the promises of God made regarding the ministry of word and sacrament. Cf. Martin E. Marty's comments quoted by Schuller in the introduction to *Self-Esteem: The New Reformation* (Waco, Tex.: Word, 1982), 11–12, and Schuller's reply as prima facie evidence.

Chapter 2: Undercurrents of Individualism

1. Robert Bellah et al., *Habits of the Heart: Individualism and Commitment in American Life* (Berkeley: University of California Press, 1985), 334.

2. Ibid., 336.

3. Ibid., 334.

4. Kennon L. Callahan, *Twelve Keys to an Effective Church: Strategic Planning for Mission* (San Francisco: Harper and Row, 1983), 35–39.

5. Ann Douglas, *The Feminization of American Culture* (New York: Avon Books, 1977), 4.

6. Wayne C. Booth, *Modern Dogma and the Rhetoric of Assent* (Chicago: University of Chicago Press, 1974), 12–14.

7. Karl Popper, *The Open Society and Its Enemies* (London: Routledge and Kegan Paul, 1947), 53.

8. Booth, *Modern Dogma,* 17–18.

9. John Locke is one important source for this bifurcation, which is built into his epistemology. For a discussion of Locke's conception of the public and private with respect to the role of women, see Jean Bethke Elshtain, *Public Man, Private Woman: Women in Social and Political Thought* (Princeton: Princeton University Press, 1981), 118ff.

10. See Elshtain, *Public Man,* 135, for a discussion of this theme, especially with regard to John Stuart Mill.

11. Henry S. Randall, "Thomas Jefferson to Henry S. Randall," undated, in *The Life of Thomas Jefferson* (New York, 1858), 3:672.

Chapter 3: Undercurrents and Liturgical Renewal

1. R. W. Franklin, *Nineteenth-Century Churches: The History of a New Catholicism in Wuerttemberg, England, and France.* (New York and London: Garland Pub. Inc., 1987), 1.

2. Ibid. Newman converted to Roman Catholicism and later became a cardinal.

3. Franklin dates the effect of Moehler's reform to the Protestant attack in September 1833 upon his *Symbolik oder Darstellun der dogmatischen Gegensatze der Katholiken und Protestanten nach ihren offentlichen Bekenntnisschriften,* published in 1832; ibid., 2.

4. George R. Muenich, "Der Haupgottesdienst in der lutherishcen Kirche Amerikas" (Diss., University of Erlangen, 1973), 6–12; Luther D. Reed, *Lutheran Liturgy,* 153.

5. James F. White, *Protestant Worship: Traditions in Transition* (Louisville: Westminster/John Knox; 1989), 53–54.

6. Ibid., 54.

7. James F. White, *Christian Worship in Transition.* (Nashville: Abingdon, 1976), 98–99.

8. Ibid., 99.

9. Ibid.

10. Ibid., 98.

11. Franklin, *Nineteenth-Century Churches,* 2.

12. Ibid., 5.

13. Ibid., 474.

14. My debt to Henry Horn, not only in this chapter, is insufficiently addressed by an endnote; his reflections remain a guiding stimulus for my own work.

15. See Louis Boyer, *Newman: His Life and Spirituality,* trans. J. Lewis May (New York: Meridian Books, 1960), and Ian Kerr, *John Henry Newman* (Oxford: Clarendon, 1991).

16. James F. White, *The Cambridge Movement: The Ecclesiologists and the Gothic Revival* (Cambridge: Cambridge University Press, 1962).

17. J. A. Moehler, "Uber die neueste Bekaempfung der Kathllischen Kirche," *Gesammelte Schriften,* 2 (Regensburg, 1839–1840), 229; as cited in ibid., 9.

18. Ibid.

19. Luther D. Reed, *The Lutheran Liturgy* (Philadelphia: Fortress Press, 1947), 162; Muenich, "Der Hauptgottesdienst, 9.

20. Carl S. Meyer, ed., *Moving Frontiers* (St. Louis: Concordia, 1964), 90–124; Muenich, "Der Hauptgottesdienst," 6–12; Reed, *Lutheran Liturgy,* 153; Wilhelm Loehe, *Three Books concerning the Church* (Reading, Penn.: Pilger Publishing House, 1908).

21. White, *Christian Worship,* 125.

22. Todd Nichol, "Liturgical Civility, Upward Mobility, and American Modernity," in *Word and World* 3 (Spring 1983): 168–77.

23. White, *Christian Worship,* 80–82.

24. Eugene L. Brand, "Worship in the Perspective of World Lutheranism," *Currents in Theology and Mission* 8, no. 3 (June 1981): 132–40.

25. Stephen Neill, *A History of Christian Missions* (Harmondsworth, Middlesex, England: Penguin Books, 1964), 553.

26. Gregory Dix, *The Shape of the Liturgy* (Glasgow: University of Glasgow Press, 1945), 142.

27. Gregor Siefer, *Church and Industrial Society* (London: Darton, Longman, and Todd, 1960); John Petrie [pseud.], trans., *The Worker-Priests: A Collective Documentation* (London: Routledge and Kegan Paul, 1956); and White, *Christian Worship,* 104–25.

28. Richard Palmer, *Hermeneutics* (Evanston, Ill.: Northwestern University Press, 1969), 75–79. This method predominates liturgical criticism as well as biblical criticism under the title "historical-critical method."

29. Geoffrey Wainwright, *Doxology: The Praise of God in Worship, Doctrine, and Life* (New York: Oxford University Press, 1980), 218ff.

30. For the text, see *The Apostolic Tradition of Hippolytus,* ed. Burton Scott Easton (Hamden, Conn.: Archon Books, 1962), 41–49.

31. White, *Christian Worship,* 102.

32. White, *Christian Worship,* 129.

33. This favorite saying of Jaroslav Pelikan is published most recently in his *Vindication of Tradition* (New Haven: Yale University Press, 1984), 65.

34. Johannes-Baptist Metz, "Relationship to Church and World in Light of Political Theology," in *Theology of Renewal,* ed. L. K. Shook (New York: Herder and Herder, 1968), 2:260.

Chapter 4: The Stranger and the Self-Giving God

1. In chapters nine and ten I discuss the role of Scripture in the model used in this book and proposed as a model for worship planning. In this chapter

I practice what I preach in those chapters. Without making extensive comment regarding the interpretive methods used here, I would simply draw attention to the following sources for the method followed in this chapter. Stanley Hauerwas, *Why Narrative?* (Grand Rapids, Mich.: Eerdmans, 1989); George Lindbeck, *The Nature of Doctrine* (Philadelphia: Westminster, 1984); Paul Ricoeur, *The Rule of Metaphor* (Toronto: Univ. of Toronto Press, 1977); David Tracy, *The Analogical Imagination* (New York: Crossroad, 1982); Ronald Thiemann, *Revelation as Theology* (Notre Dame, Ind.: Univ. of Notre Dame Press, 1986). Those convinced that these sources are incompatible will need to test their assumptions on how I actually interpret the biblical texts, since my intent in this volume is not to engage in the continuing debate over method between the Chicago and Yale schools, but to shape contemporary worship and evangelism within the biblical metaphor of hospitality to the stranger.

2. John Koenig, *New Testament Hospitality: Partnership with Strangers as Promise and Mission* (Philadelphia: Fortress Press, 1985), 12.

3. Robert Webber, *Celebrating Our Faith: Evangelism through Worship* (San Francisco: Harper and Row, 1986).

4. Paul Holmer, "About Liturgy and Its Logic," *Worship* 50, no. 1 (January 1976): 23.

5. Terence Fretheim, *The Suffering of God* (Philadelphia: Fortress Press, 1984), 60–65; and "Worship in Israel" (unpublished article, worship textbook, Luther Northwestern Theological Seminary, St. Paul, Minn.), 26.

6. Karl Rahner in *Foundations of Christian Faith: An Introduction to the Idea of Christianity* (New York: Crossroad, 1989), 116–37, develops this logic of God's free and forgiving self-communication and ties it to the doctrine of the Trinity; likewise, in a more developed manner, see Robert Jenson's discussion in Carl Braaten and Robert Jenson, *Christian Dogmatics,* vol. 2, (Philadelphia: Fortress Press, 1984), 291–394.

7. James F. White, *Christian Worship in Transition* (Nashville: Abingdon Press, 1976).

8. The following analysis depends on James F. White, *Sacraments as God's Self-Giving* (Nashville: Abingdon Press, 1983), 15–22.

9. Fretheim, "Worship in Israel," 29.

10. See Arland Hultgren, "Worship in the New Testament" (unpublished article, worship textbook, Luther Northwestern Theological Seminary, St. Paul, Minn.).

11. Jean Daniélou, *The Theology of Jewish Christianity* (Chicago: H. Regnery, 1964).

12. Donald Juel, *Messiah and Temple* (Chico, Calif.: Scholars Press, 1977).

13. Hultgren, "Worship in the New Testament," 10–11.

14. Koenig, *New Testament Hospitality,* 26.

15. Ibid., 32.

16. Elisabeth Schüssler Fiorenza, *In Memory of Her: A Feminist Theological Reconstruction of Christian Origins* (New York: Crossroad, 1983), 145–47. She cites Mark 3:31-35; 10:29; Matt. 10:34-36/Luke 12:51-53.

17. Arthur McGill develops this same insight from Luke and shows how it leads to the doctrine of the Trinity in his deceptively simple book *Suffering: A Test of Theological Method* (Philadelphia: Geneva Press, 1968), 47–75.

18. Koenig, *New Testament Hospitality*, 90.

19. Ibid., 52–84.

20. Gerd Theissen, *The Social Setting of Pauline Christianity: Essays on Corinth*, trans. J. H. Schütz (Philadelphia: Fortress Press, 1982), esp. "Social Integration and Sacramental Activity: An Analysis of 1 Cor. 11:17-34," 145–74.

21. Koenig, *New Testament Hospitality*, 60.

22. Theissen, *Social Setting*, 151–63, as cited in Koenig, *New Testament Hospitality*, 67.

23. 1 Peter develops the theme of Christians as resident aliens, strangers in a strange land; cf. John Elliot, *A Home for the Homeless: A Sociological Exegesis of 1 Peter, Its Situation and Strategy* (Philadelphia: Fortress, 1981) and Elliot's *1 Peter: Estrangement and Community* (Chicago: Franciscan Herald Press, 1979).

24. George F. Moore, *Judaism in the First Centuries of the Christian Era* (Cambridge, Mass.: Harvard Univ. Press, 1927–30), 1:291–307, as cited in Hultgren, "Worship in the New Testament," 12.

25. Koenig, *New Testament Hospitality*, 119.

26. *The Apostolic Tradition of Hippolytus*, ed. Burton Scott Easton (Hamden, Conn.: Archon Books, 1962).

27. Cited in David J. Bosch, *Witness to the World: The Christian Mission in Theological Perspective* (Atlanta, Ga.: John Knox Press, 1980), 199.

Chapter 5: A Gospel-Centered Public Worship

1. By "within the biblical metaphor," I mean specifically that this metaphor does not illustrate some other and universal abstraction but is the metaphor within which other images are being developed. As such I do not believe that I master the metaphor of hospitality to the stranger but that I am its pupil; it seizes me rather than I it. Paul Ricoeur discusses this phenonmenon of being seized rather than seizing, especially regarding the question of referentiality in his book *The Rule of Metaphor* (Toronto: Univ. of Toronto Press, 1977), 254. It is this theory of metaphorical and narrative truth that informs this chapter in particular, and the book in general.

2. This chapter is indebted to the work of Emmanuel Levinas, especially "Beyond Intentionality," in *Philosophy in France Today*, ed. Alan Montefiore (Cambridge: Cambridge Univ. Press, 1983), 112–13; *Totality and Infinity*, trans. A. Lingis (Pittsburgh: Duquesne Univ. Press, 1969); *Otherwise than*

Being or Beyond Essence, trans. A. Lingis (The Hague: Martinus Nijhoff, 1981); and *The Levinas Reader: Emmanuel Levinas,* ed. Sean Hand (Cambridge: Basil Blackwell, 1989); see also Alfred Schutz, *The Phenomenology of the Social World* (Evanston, Ill.: Northwestern Univ. Press, 1967), 163–71.

3. Levinas, "Beyond Intentionality," 112–13.

4. *Face to Face with Levinas,* ed. R. Cohen (Albany: SUNY Press, 1986), 27.

5. Levinas, "God and Philosophy," in *Reader,* 184.

6. Gustaf Wingren, *Credo: The Christian View of Faith and Life,* trans. Edgar M. Carlson (Minneapolis: Augsburg, 1981), as in other places, makes a similar argument regarding the urging and compelling of God's law through the moral summons of the neighbor.

7. Levinas argues: "The first consciousness of my immorality is not my subordination to facts, but to the Other" (*Totality,* 83); "The Other imposes himself as an exigency that dominates this freedom, and hence as more primordial than everything that takes place in me" (*Totality,* 87); "The Other commands and judges" (*Totality,* 87).

Some feminist scholars—to my knowledge, only Christian and post-Christian ones, in marked contrast to Jewish feminist scholarship—take strong exception to this command language in Levinas's interpretation; see, for example, Sharon Welch, *A Feminist Ethic of Risk* (Minneapolis: Fortress Press, 1990), 163–64.

8. Thomas W. Ogletree, *Hospitality to the Stranger* (Philadelphia: Fortress Press, 1985).

9. Jean-Paul Sartre, *Being and Nothingness* (New York: Philosophical Library, 1956), 259–62.

10. On the relation between truth and justice, see Levinas, *Totality,* 82-101; "Ethics as First Philosophy," in *Reader,* 75–87.

11. Saul Bellow, *Dangling Man* (New York: Vanguard Press, 1944).

12. Ogletree, *Hospitality,* 46.

13. Levinas, *Totality,* 26. The eschatological dimension of Levinas's analysis of the face-to-face encounter is of critical significance for theology, especially a theology of public life. The overall proposal made in this book is thoroughly formed with a view toward recovering the eschatological character of the biblical narrative and the Christian gospel.

14. See the work of Alfred Schutz on structuring the interaction of strangers and his concept of people groups, esp. "The Stranger: An Essay in Social Psychology," in *Collected Papers,* ed. Arvid Brodersen (The Hague: Martinus Nijhoff, 1964), 2:91–105; and *The Structures of the Life-World* (Evanston, Ill.: Northwestern Univ. Press, 1973), 59–72.

15. A theology of contemporary public offices and systems is especially needed.

16. Claus Westermann, *Blessing in the Bible and the Life of the Church,* trans. Keith Crim (Philadelphia: Fortress Press, 1978), was among the first biblical scholars in the postwar period to make this observation.

17. Claus Westermann, *Genesis 1–11: A Commentary,* trans. John J. Scullion, S.J., Continental Commentary series (Minneapolis: Augsburg, 1984), 139–77.

18. Gustaf Wingren, *Credo;* also *Creation and Law,* trans. Ross Mackenzie (Edinburgh: Oliver and Boyd, 1961); and *Luther on Vocation,* trans. Carl C. Rasmussen (Philadelphia: Muhlenberg Press, 1957).

19. A connection can be drawn between the irrelevance to many modern theologians of the doctrine of the Trinity and the bondage of contemporary culture and theology to the totalizing "I." This relationship has been explored to some extent by the new Trinitarian theologians, esp. Robert W. Jenson, *Triune Identity* (Philadelphia: Fortress Press, 1982), and Eberhard Jüngel, *God as the Mystery of the World,* trans. Darrell L. Guder (Grand Rapids, Mich.: Eerdmans, 1983). The significance of the doctrine of the Trinity for a theology of public life, however, still needs further development.

20. See, for example, Carol Gilligan, *In a Different Voice: Psychological Theory and Women's Development* (Cambridge, Mass.: Harvard University Press, 1982); and *Mapping the Moral Domain: A Contribution of Women's Thinking to Psychological Theory and Education* (Cambridge, Mass.: Harvard University Press, 1988).

21. See, for example, Jürgen Habermas, *Communication and the Evolution of Society,* trans. Thomas McCarthy (Boston: Beacon Press, 1979); and *Knowledge and Human Interests,* trans. Jeremy J. Shapiro (London: Heinemann Educational, 1978).

22. Delbert Hillers, *Covenant: The History of a Biblical Idea* (Baltimore: Johns Hopkins University Press, 1969).

23. Gerhard Forde, *The Law-Gospel Debate: An Interpretation of Its Historical Development* (Minneapolis: Augsburg, 1969), 49–68; also "The Work of Christ," in *Christian Dogmatics* (Philadelphia: Fortress Press, 1984), 79–99.

24. Arthur McGill, *Suffering: A Test of Theological Method* (Philadelphia: Westminster Press, 1982).

25. Jüngel, *God as the Mystery,* 184–225.

26. See Wolfhart Pannenberg, *Jesus—God and Man,* trans. Lewis L. Wilkins and Duane A. Priebe (Philadelphia: Westminster Press, 1977), 74ff., for a discussion of the difference between the various analogies for resurrection and the historical claims associated with each one.

27. John D. Zizioulas, *Being as Communion* (Crestwood, N.Y.: St. Vladimir's, 1985), 110–22.

28. Aidan Kavanagh, *The Shape of Baptism: The Rite of Christian Initiation* (New York: Pueblo, 1978).

29. On manifestation and proclamation, see David Tracy, *Analogical Imagination* (New York: Crossroad, 1982), 202–18; and Paul Ricoeur, "Manifestation and Proclamation," *The Journal of the Blaisdell Institute* 12 (Winter 1978).

30. Richard Norris and Aidan Kavanagh, O.S.B., *The Baptismal Mystery and the Catechumenate* (New York: The Church Hymnal Corp., 1990).

31. Cf. Gerhard O. Forde, *Theology Is for Proclamation* (Minneapolis: Fortress Press, 1990).

32. Marc Kolden, in "Cleaning Up Our Language about Ministry," in *dialog* 25, no. 1, pp. 33–38, clarifies this matter of the unique ministry of the church.

33. Geoffrey Wainwright, *Doxology: The Praise of God in Worship, Doctrine, and Life* (New York: Oxford University Press, 1980), 12.

34. A notable exception in the pastoral-care movement is Don S. Browning, *Religious Ethics and Pastoral Care,* Theology and Pastoral Care series (Philadelphia: Fortress Press, 1982).

35. Sheryl Kleinmann, *Equals before God: Seminarians as Humanistic Professionals* (Chicago: University of Chicago Press, 1979).

36. Martin Luther King, Jr., *Strength to Love,* reprint (Philadelphia: Fortress Press, 1981).

37. Eg., Kenneth Haugt, *Christian Caregiving: A Way of Life* (Minneapolis: Augsburg, 1984) and its *Leader's Guide* (Minneapolis: Augsburg, 1986).

Chapter 6: Liturgical Evangelism

1. Robert Webber, *Celebrating Our Faith: Evangelism through Worship* (San Francisco: Harper and Row, 1986), 13. Cf. Aidan Kavanagh, *Initiation Theology* (Toronto: The Anglican Book Center, 1978); *Confirmation: Origins and Reform* (New York: Pueblo, 1978); *The Shape of Baptism: The Rite of Christian Initiation* (New York: Pueblo, 1978); and Lawrence E. Mick, *Renewing the Church as an Initiating Assembly* (Collegeville, Minn.: Liturgical Press, 1989).

2. Webber, *Celebrating Our Faith,* 3.

3. Ibid., 79.

4. Ibid., 3.

5. *The Apostolic Tradition of Hippolytus,* ed. Burton Scott Easton (Hamden, Conn.: Archon Books, 1962).

6. *Rite of Christian Initiation of Adults* (Collegeville, Minn.: Liturgical Press, 1988), 77.

7. Ibid., 79.

Chapter 7: Ritual as Hospitality

1. Cf. Richard Sennett's most complete and recent discussion of architecture in contemporary urban culture in *The Conscience of the Eye: The Design and Social Life of Cities* (New York: Alfred A. Knopf, 1990).

2. Richard Sennett, *The Fall of Public Man: On the Social Psychology of Capitalism* (New York: Random House, 1978), 15.

3. Ibid., 266.

4. Ibid.

5. Ibid., 92–93; 264–65. See also Erik Erikson, *Toys and Reasons* (New York: W. W. Norton, 1977), esp. on ambivalence and distance, 88ff.

Chapter 8: Ritual Strategies

1. See Roland A. Delattre, "Ritual Resourcefulness and Cultural Pluralism," *Soundings* 41, no. 3 (1978): 281–301. This article has greatly influenced the following analysis.

2. Mark Searle, *Liturgy Made Simple* (Collegeville, Minn.: Liturgical Press, 1981; Gail Ramshaw, *Christ in Sacred Speech* (Philadelphia: Fortress Press, 1986).

3. George Lindbeck, The *Nature of Doctrine* (Philadelphia: Westminster, 1984).

4. Charles Black, Jr., *Capital Punishment: The Inevitability of Caprice and Mistake,* 2nd ed. (New York: Norton, 1981). Black documents the capricious character of capital punishment before and after the Supreme Court's rulings of 1976.

5. Klaus Hansen, *Mormonism and American Experience* (Chicago: University of Chicago Press, 1982).

6. Gail Sheehy, *Passages: Predictable Crises of Adult Life* (New York: Dutton, 1974).

7. Elizabeth Kübler-Ross, *Death and Dying* (New York: Macmillan, 1969).

8. See Daniel J. Simundson, *Faith under Fire: Biblical Interpretations of Suffering* (Minneapolis: Augsburg, 1980), 43–62; and Donald Capps, *Biblical Approaches to Pastoral Counseling* (Philadelphia: Westminster Press, 1981). *Interpretation* 28 (January 1974) is dedicated entirely to articles on laments.

9. Elaine Ramshaw, in *Ritual and Pastoral Care,* Theology and Pastoral Care series (Philadelphia: Fortress Press, 1987), does an unequaled job of introducing this critical topic.

Chapter 9: A Public Imagination

1. Richard Sennett, *The Fall of Public Man: On the Social Psychology of Capitalism* (New York: Random House, 1978), 64–87.

2. Elaine Ramshaw, *Ritual and Pastoral Care,* Theology and Pastoral Care series (Philadelphia: Fortress Press, 1987), 25–28.

3. Kennon L. Callahan, *Twelve Keys to an Effective Church: Strategic Planning for Mission* (San Francisco: Harper and Row, 1983).

4. Callahan, *Twelve Keys.*

5. Pierre Babin, *The New Era in Religious Communication,* with Mercedes Iannone, trans. David Smith (Minneapolis: Fortress Press, 1991), 168–81.

Chapter 10: Planning Public Worship

1. Robert L. Wilson, *Shaping the Congregation* (Nashville: Abingdon Press, 1981), 1.

2. Regarding discrimens, see David Kelsey, *The Uses of Scripture in Recent Theology* (Philadelphia: Fortress Press, 1975) 160ff.; and Robert Johnson, *Authority in Protestant Theology* (Philadelphia: Westminster Press, 1959). Regarding metaphor, see George Lakoff and Mark Johnson, *Metaphors We Live By* (Chicago: University of Chicago Press, 1980); and Paul Ricoeur, *The Rule of Metaphor* (Toronto: University of Toronto Press, 1977).

3. For a fuller discussion of these three elements, see Patrick R. Keifert, "Truth and Taste on Sunday Morning," in *dialog* 25, no. 3, pp. 193–200; the following exposition is deeply indebted to James and Evelyn Whitehead, *Method in Ministry* (New York: Seabury, 1981), and Bernard Lonergan, S.J., *Method in Theology* (New York: Herder and Herder, 1972).

4. See esp. Juan Luis Segundo, *Theology and the Church: A Response to Cardinal Ratzinger and a Warning to the Whole Church*, trans. J. W. Diereksmeier (Minneapolis: Winston Press, 1985); and Ricoeur, *Rule of Metaphor*.